Getting Started with Microsoft Power Pages

Build, Customize, and Manage Secure External Web Solutions

Dr. Gomathi S
Jerald Felix

Apress®

Getting Started with Microsoft Power Pages: Build, Customize, and Manage Secure External Web Solutions

Dr. Gomathi S
BSR GLN Apartment, A1, Block 4
Chennai, Tamil Nadu, India

Jerald Felix
Coimbatore, Tamil Nadu, India

ISBN-13 (pbk): 979-8-8688-2666-5
https://doi.org/10.1007/979-8-8688-2667-2

ISBN-13 (electronic): 979-8-8688-2667-2

Managing Director, Apress Media LLC: Welmoed Spahr
Acquisitions Editor: Smriti Srivastava
Editorial Assistant: Marina Engler

Cover designed by eStudioCalamar

Distributed to the book trade worldwide by Springer Science+Business Media New York, 1 New York Plaza, New York, NY 10004. Phone 1-800-SPRINGER, fax (201) 348-4505, e-mail orders-ny@springer-sbm.com, or visit www.springeronline.com. Apress Media, LLC is a Delaware LLC and the sole member (owner) is Springer Science + Business Media Finance Inc (SSBM Finance Inc). SSBM Finance Inc is a **Delaware** corporation.

For information on translations, please e-mail booktranslations@springernature.com; for reprint, paperback, or audio rights, please e-mail bookpermissions@springernature.com.

Apress titles may be purchased in bulk for academic, corporate, or promotional use. eBook versions and licenses are also available for most titles. For more information, reference our Print and eBook Bulk Sales web page at http://www.apress.com/bulk-sales.

Any source code or other supplementary material referenced by the author in this book is available to readers on GitHub. For more detailed information, please visit https://www.apress.com/gp/services/source-code.

If disposing of this product, please recycle the paper

Table of Contents

About the Authors

Dr. Gomathi S is a Microsoft Most Valuable Professional (MVP), Microsoft Certified Trainer (MCT), Community Lead, and Microsoft Learn Expert with deep expertise in AI, Power Platform, and data analytics. She currently works as an AI Technical Trainer, helping professionals and organizations adopt AI-driven solutions using Microsoft technologies. With a Ph.D. in Computer Science specializing in Data Mining, Dr. Gomathi combines strong academic foundations with extensive hands-on industry experience. She has trained thousands of professionals and students on Microsoft Power BI, Power Platform, Copilot, and AI-enabled analytics, enabling learners to build practical, real-world solutions. Dr. Gomathi is an active contributor to the global Microsoft community, regularly speaking at technical events and mentoring learners through structured training programs. Her work focuses on simplifying complex AI and low-code concepts and empowering professionals to build secure, scalable, and intelligent business solutions.

Jerald Louis Raja Nicholas Anto Felix is a Microsoft Certified Trainer (MCT) community lead and Power Platform Super User with over five years of experience empowering learners and professionals through Microsoft technologies. He has been working in IT for more than a decade. Jerald has delivered impactful sessions on Azure, Power Platform, and AI solutions to a diverse audience ranging from students to IT professionals. He is an active member of the global Microsoft community, contributing as a speaker at events such as Azure Global Bootcamp and various MCT meetups, while also creating Tamil learning resources on YouTube to make advanced cloud and AI concepts accessible to regional communities. His dedication to technical education is reflected in his certifications spanning Azure AI, Data, Security, and Copilot technologies.

About the Technical Reviewer

Naga Santhosh Reddy Vootukuri is a Principal Software Engineering Manager at Microsoft, working within the Cloud Computing + AI (C+AI) organization. With over 17 years of experience spanning across three countries (India, China, and the United States), Naga has developed a rich and varied technical background. His expertise lies in Cloud Computing, Artificial Intelligence, distributed systems, and microservices.

At Microsoft, Naga leads the Azure SQL Database team, focusing on optimizing SQL deployment processes to enhance the efficiency and scalability of services for millions of databases globally. He is responsible for the entire infrastructure of the Azure SQL deployment space and has been instrumental in the development of Master Data Services, a master data management solution by Microsoft. This project earned him recognition for delivering impactful solutions to complex data challenges.

Naga has authored and published numerous research articles in peer-reviewed and indexed journals. He is the author of three books which are well recognized in the developer community. He is a Senior Member of IEEE, Docker captain, and Dapr Meteor and contributes to writing technical articles as a Core MVB member at DZone, engaging with millions of active readers. He also serves as an editorial board member for a highly reputed science journal (SCI), where he reviews research articles on Cloud Computing and AI.

In addition to his professional roles, Naga is deeply involved in the tech community as a speaker, book reviewer for Apress, and contributor to platforms like DZone and the Microsoft Tech Community. He recently served as IEEE AI summit Committee chair and lightning talk chair and selected some of the best lightning talks. He also served at IEEE cloud summit 2026 as Industry cloud chair. He has delivered AI-related workshops and received an AI innovator award from Washington Senator Lisa Wellman. He also served as a judge for multiple hackathons like Fabric AI hackathon and Cosmos DB AI hackathon on Devpost, which further showcased his expertise and commitment to the advancement of technology.

Acknowledgments

Writing this book has been a deeply meaningful journey—one that would not have been possible without the support, encouragement, and inspiration of many remarkable people.

I dedicate this book to my beloved **mother, Janaki,** whose memory continues to inspire me every day. Though she is no longer with us, her love, strength, and values live on in everything I do.

To my **father, Srinivasan**, thank you for being my role model and for instilling in me a passion for learning and perseverance. To my **husband, Anantha Krishnan,** your unwavering support, encouragement, and thoughtful guidance made this journey so much more fulfilling. I am equally thankful to my **brother, Viswanathan**, for his constant support.

A special mention goes to my cute **twin boys, Vishanth and Vishwanth,** whose playful energy, love, and even their little acts of mischief brought joy and balance to my days, helping me stay grounded and motivated throughout the writing process.

Introduction

Modern organizations increasingly require secure, scalable, and user-friendly web portals to interact with customers, partners, employees, and external stakeholders. Traditionally, building such portals required extensive development effort, complex infrastructure management, and specialized programming skills. With the evolution of low-code platforms, organizations can now create powerful web applications and portals with significantly reduced development time.

Microsoft Power Pages, a part of the Microsoft Power Platform, enables organizations to design, build, and deploy secure external-facing websites using a low-code approach. It allows both developers and non-developers to create modern web experiences while seamlessly integrating with Microsoft Dataverse, Power Automate, Power BI, and other Microsoft services.

Power Pages evolved from Power Apps Portals, bringing enhanced design capabilities, improved security models, AI-assisted development with Copilot, and a more intuitive design experience through the Design Studio. With Power Pages, businesses can rapidly create data-driven portals for use cases such as customer self-service portals, partner collaboration platforms, registration systems, and data submission portals.

This book is designed to provide a complete and structured learning path for building professional-grade Power Pages solutions. It guides readers from the foundational concepts to advanced customization, security implementation, and production deployment.

The goal of this book is to help readers

- Understand the core architecture and components of Power Pages

- Learn how Power Pages integrates with Dataverse and the broader Power Platform ecosystem

- Build and design modern websites using low-code tools and AI-powered Copilot capabilities

- Implement data-driven forms, lists, and multi-step processes

- Extend Power Pages with developer tools such as Liquid templates, JavaScript, and APIs

- Configure security, authentication, and governance practices

- Deploy and manage Power Pages solutions in enterprise environments

The book follows a step-by-step practical approach, combining conceptual explanations with guided exercises to help readers gain hands-on experience.

You will begin by understanding the fundamentals of Power Pages, including architecture, components, and environment setup. The book then walks through designing and building sites using the Design Studio and Copilot. As you progress, you will explore how to connect Power Pages to data sources, create dynamic forms and lists, and integrate with other Power Platform services.

Later chapters focus on advanced customization and developer extensions, allowing readers to enhance portal functionality through Liquid templates, APIs, JavaScript, and Power Automate workflows. The final chapter covers security, deployment, and administration, ensuring that your Power Pages solutions are enterprise-ready.

To further support learning and practical application, the book also includes helpful appendixes covering troubleshooting checklists, terminology references, certification learning paths, interview preparation questions, and production readiness guidance.

Whether you are a Power Platform developer, functional consultant, solution architect, or IT professional, this book will help you gain the knowledge and practical skills needed to successfully design and deploy Power Pages solutions.

By the end of this book, you will have the confidence to build secure, scalable, and professionally designed websites using Microsoft Power Pages.

CHAPTER 1

Introduction to Power Pages

Chapter Objectives

In this chapter, you will gain a foundational understanding of Microsoft Power Pages, what it is, how it fits into the broader Power Platform ecosystem, and why organizations use it to build secure, data-driven websites for external users. You will explore its core capabilities, from low-code design and responsive site creation to pro-developer extensibility using Liquid, Web APIs, and advanced tooling.

The chapter introduces the key architectural components of a Power Pages solution, including sites, Dataverse tables, web roles, and web files, and explains how authentication and authorization work together to protect data. You will also learn about the history and evolution of Power Pages from earlier portal technologies, understand important governance and compliance principles such as the role of administrators and ALM, and complete the essential environment setup steps, licensing, provisioning a trial or developer environment, and enabling Dataverse. By the end of this chapter, you will be fully prepared to begin building your first Power Pages site with confidence.

What Is Power Pages?

Microsoft Power Pages is a secure, low-code, enterprise-grade website builder that enables you to create, host, and manage external-facing business websites, all integrated with your organization's data stored in Microsoft Dataverse.

© Dr. Gomathi S, Jerald Felix 2026
Dr. Gomathi S and J. Felix, *Getting Started with Microsoft Power Pages*,
https://doi.org/10.1007/979-8-8688-2667-2_1

It is part of the Microsoft Power Platform, alongside Power Apps, Power Automate, Power BI, and Power Virtual Agents, giving businesses a unified ecosystem for app development, automation, analytics, and customer engagement.

Power Pages empowers both **citizen developers** (non-technical users) and **professional developers** to

- **Design** responsive websites quickly using templates or a drag-and-drop design studio

- **Integrate** data securely from Dataverse, Dynamics 365, or other data sources

- **Collaborate** with developers using Visual Studio Code, GitHub, and Power Platform CLI for advanced customization

- **Automate** workflows using Power Automate and embed reports using Power BI

Key Features

Power Pages brings together a blend of intuitive design tools and enterprise-grade capabilities. Table 1-1 highlights its key features that make it a powerful platform for building secure, data-driven websites.

Table 1-1. *Key Features of Microsoft Power Pages*

Feature	Description
Design Studio	A user-friendly, no-code interface for designing pages, layouts, and themes
Templates Hub	Ready-to-use website templates for portals like customer self-service, community sites, and partner portals
Secure Access	Role-based authentication through Azure AD, Microsoft Entra ID, or other identity providers
Dataverse Integration	Store, manage, and display structured business data easily and securely
Pro-Developer Tools	Extend websites with HTML, CSS, JavaScript, Liquid templates, and Web APIs
Responsive Design	Websites automatically adapt to mobile, tablet, and desktop devices
Built-in Analytics	Monitor site performance and user engagement using Microsoft analytics tools

Core Purpose and Access

- **External Websites:** Power Pages allows organizations to build and launch websites that are accessible to external users.

- **User Identity and Access:** The websites support users signing in using a wide variety of identities. They can also be configured to allow users to browse content anonymously.

- **Data Interaction:** A primary function of Power Pages is to allow users to create and view data in Dataverse. Power Pages extends Dataverse capabilities, allowing external users to create, update, and view Dataverse information.

Design, Building, and Development

Power Pages provides comprehensive tools for both low-code makers and professional developers:

- **Low-Code Design**: Sites can be created using the new design studio. Makers utilize the Pages workspace to create and design pages, and the Styling workspace to theme and style the site and set up their brand kit. Sites can also be created using templates.

- **Data Component Integration**: Users can add various data components to pages, including lists, basic forms, and multistep forms. The data workspace is available for managing this integration.

- **Professional Development**: For advanced customization, developers can use specialized tools and methods, such as Liquid, Web templates, the Portals web API, and Code components. It is also possible to configure Power Automate cloud flows within the site. Alternatively, developers can utilize the Portal Management app and Visual Studio Code and Power Platform CLI.

Tip   Before you start building, clearly define your website's purpose, whether it's for customers, partners, or community members. This helps you decide what data needs to be shared, what authentication method to use, and how to organize your pages effectively.

Security and Administration

Protecting sites and data is a critical aspect of Power Pages.

- **Security Configuration**: Power Pages administrators can set up authentication and protect data by configuring web roles and table permissions.

- **Architecture and Security White Papers**: Documentation is available covering the architecture and security white papers for Power Pages.

- **Data Loss Prevention (DLP)**: Administrators can enforce additional security measures via a Data Loss Prevention policy. This policy can be configured from the Power Platform Admin Center and aims to block anonymous access to data in Dataverse tables via Power Pages. This prevents makers from unintentionally exposing organizational data to anonymous users by enforcing authentication for all end users.

- **Administration**: Management tasks are handled through the portal's admin center, which also facilitates troubleshooting and diagnostics and reviewing consumption.

Important   Always configure security early in your design process. Properly set up web roles, table permissions, and Data Loss Prevention policies to ensure external users can only access the information they are authorized to see. Neglecting these controls can lead to unintended data exposure.

Advanced Features and Ecosystem

- **AI and Copilot**: Power Pages incorporates AI-powered and Copilot features to accelerate development, allowing makers to create AI-generated forms, add AI-generated text, and enable an agent in their site.

- **Application Lifecycle Management (ALM)**: Power Pages is designed to support ALM. With solution awareness for Power Pages, site configuration becomes portable, making it effortless to migrate the site and its components between environments. This capability provides a simplified and enhanced visual experience for managing Power Pages components.

- **Power Platform Context**: Power Pages operates within the larger Power Platform ecosystem, which is a comprehensive resource that also includes Power Apps (for low-code apps), Power Automate (for automated workflows), and Power BI (for interactive insights). Power Pages can be placed right at the center of the decision support solution.

History: From Power Apps Portals to Power Pages

Origins: Power Apps Portals

The concept began as an external-facing web/portal capability in the context of the Dynamics 365 Portals offering, enabling organizations to expose data in Microsoft Dataverse (and the underlying Common Data Service) to external users via a website. Over time, this capability became integrated into Power Apps and labeled "Power Apps Portals."

For example, the documentation for portals in the context of Finance and Operations mentions "Power Apps Portals" as the portal solution. Also, release-plan documents refer to "Power Apps Portals" features across waves.

Thus, "Power Apps Portals" became the working name for Microsoft's low-code external-site solution built on Dataverse.

Evolution and Re-branding to Power Pages

As the Power Platform matured, Microsoft surfaced a more dedicated portal/website product with enhanced low-code site-builder experiences, a refreshed licensing approach, and a clearer branded identity. That product is Power Pages.

As shown in Figure 1-1, Microsoft's portal technology has undergone several significant transitions, progressing from Dynamics 365 Portals to Power Apps Portals and eventually evolving into Power Pages through feature updates, security improvements, and the introduction of a modern administrative experience.

Figure 1-1. *Evolution of Power Apps Portals*

Key Milestones

- **Pre-2020 (approx)**: Dynamics 365 Portals → Power Apps Portals: The portal technology originally part of Dynamics 365 becomes available via Power Apps and the broader Power Platform ecosystem.

- **2021/2022**: Continuous feature enhancements to portals. For instance, the 2021 Wave 2 release plan lists new "Power Apps Portals" features (Choices multi-select columns, portals Web API support, PWA support) in September/October 2021.

- **October 2022**: With website version 9.4.9.xx, new sites created in "Power Pages or Power Apps Portals" default to private mode (indicating a shift toward the Power Pages brand).

- **June 2023**: The Power Apps Portals admin center is deprecated; the Power Pages admin hub becomes the supported experience.

- **January 2025**: The "What is Power Pages?" article reflects the branding and positioning of Power Pages as a mature, standalone offering.

Why the Change?

- **Branding Clarity**: "Portals" had been the terminology for years; moving to "Pages" aligns better with the idea of low-code websites/pages rather than just portals.

- **Product Focus**: Power Pages emphasizes a dedicated website builder experience (templates, design studio, hosting) for both internal and external audiences, while integrating tightly with Dataverse and the Power Platform.

- **Governance, Security, and Licensing**: The shift included updated admin experience, protected site creation defaults, and changed licensing models.

Current State

Today, Power Pages is the main offering for building secure, responsive, data-driven websites on the Power Platform. The documentation emphasizes that Power Pages is the newest member of the Power Platform family, and that it uses the same shared business data platform (Dataverse) used by other Power Platform components.

While "Power Apps Portals" remains in legacy documentation contexts, the active investment and product evolution is focused on Power Pages.

When and Why to Use Power Pages

Power Pages is the right choice when you need to build a **secure, data-driven website** that connects people outside your organization, such as customers, partners, or vendors, with your business data.

You might use it when you want to

- Allow customers to **submit forms**, track applications, or view personalized data online

- Enable partners or suppliers to **access shared business information** safely

- Publish a **responsive website** that works across devices, without having to write complex code

- Create a **portal experience** that connects directly to your Dataverse data or other Power Platform solutions

- Manage your websites and data from the **same environment** where you already build apps, automate workflows, or create reports

In short, you use Power Pages whenever you want to **bridge the gap between your internal data and the people who need to interact with it externally**, all within the Microsoft Power Platform ecosystem.

Why Use Power Pages

Power Pages exists to make **professional-grade web development simple, secure, and accessible.** It combines the flexibility of traditional web design with the ease of low-code tools, empowering both business users and developers to work together. As illustrated in Figure 1-2, Power Pages brings together a set of powerful features, from unified Dataverse data integration and enterprise security to low-code design, responsiveness, and tight Power Platform connectivity, that enable organizations to build modern, data-driven websites quickly and securely.

Here's why it matters:

- **Unified Data Foundation**

  Power Pages is built on Microsoft Dataverse, the same data backbone used by Power Apps, Power Automate, and Power BI. This means your website doesn't just display data, it becomes part of your entire digital ecosystem, keeping everything consistent and connected.

- **Low-Code, High-Impact Design**

  You don't need to be a web developer to build in Power Pages. Its visual design studio, templates, and drag-and-drop features let you design quickly while maintaining a professional finish.

- **Security First**

  Every site created with Power Pages inherits the enterprise-grade security, compliance, and role-based access controls of the Microsoft Cloud. You decide who can view, edit, or contribute data, ensuring full control over sensitive information.

- **Integration Across the Power Platform**

  Power Pages doesn't stand alone. It connects seamlessly with Power Automate for workflows, Power BI for data visualizations, and Power Apps for app logic, giving you the ability to create end-to-end business solutions that extend beyond a single tool.

- **Responsive and Scalable**

  Sites built with Power Pages automatically adapt to any screen size. Whether you're serving 10 users or 10,000, your site remains fast, consistent, and visually polished.

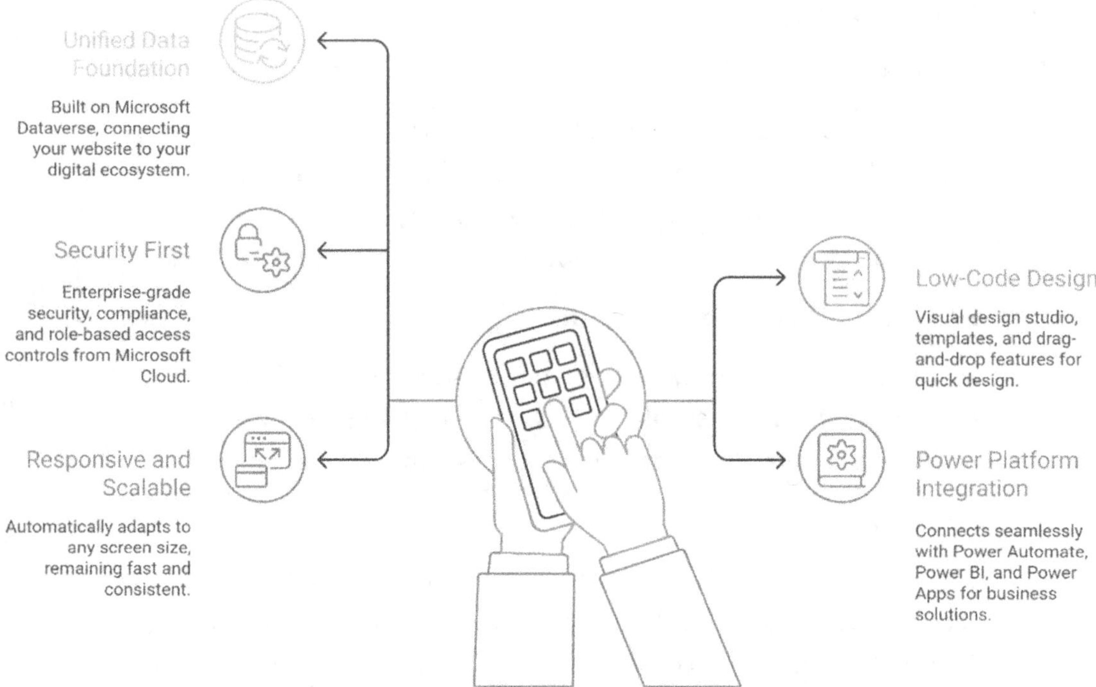

Figure 1-2. *Key Features of Microsoft Power Pages*

Use Power Pages when your business needs a secure, interactive website that works like an extension of your internal systems, not just a brochure or landing page.

Think of it as the natural next step when a Power App is no longer enough, and you need the same low-code convenience brought to the web. With Power Pages, you can turn your data into dynamic online experiences that inform, engage, and empower your audience, without leaving the comfort of the Power Platform.

Understanding Power Pages Architecture

When you begin working with Microsoft Power Pages, you're entering a world where websites connect with business data, user roles, and reusable assets. To make things clearer, let's break down its major components, what each one is, how it fits in the architecture, and what to keep in mind as you build your first site.

Sites

A *Site* in Power Pages is the website you create and publish for your users (internal or external). It is the visible interface, the pages, navigation, branding, layout, and content that people visit in a browser.

- Conceptually, the site is the *frontend* of your solution: where users land, browse, fill out forms, view lists, and interact.

- Behind the scenes, the site runs on Power Pages infrastructure: it connects to a Microsoft Dataverse database, may use web files (CSS, JavaScript, images), and obeys security models (web roles, permissions).

- As a builder, you'll work in the *Design Studio* of Power Pages: adding pages, embedding forms and lists, controlling layout, and linking to data.

Tip   Think of the "Site" as the visible, user-facing part of the architecture. Everything else supports it.

Important   Although you design the site interface, you must keep in mind underlying data, roles, and access (without which the site might display nothing or expose too much).

Dataverse

At the heart of data-driven Power Pages sites is Microsoft Dataverse. In simple terms, it's the data platform that stores your business data and configuration.

- Dataverse stores **both** the website's configuration (pages, site settings, content, snippets) *and* business data (e.g., customer records, transactions) for the site.

- You can create standard tables (predefined) and custom tables in Dataverse to capture the information your website needs. The flexibility means you define whatever fields/data you need: names, dates, status, etc.

- When you build a list or a form on your Power Pages site, often you are pulling data from Dataverse, showing it or updating it.

- Because the configuration and the data live in the same platform, things like security, relationships, and logic (business rules) can be managed consistently.

Tip   Familiarize yourself with the tables that Power Pages uses (both system and your custom ones) before building complex features.

Important   Don't ignore the performance and security aspects of Dataverse, good data modeling and permissions will make a difference in how smoothly your site runs.

Web Roles

Web roles are a mechanism in Power Pages to define *who* can do *what* on your site. They are akin to permission groups for users of the site (especially external/portal users).

- A web role defines a set of permissions tied to content, data, and pages. For example, you might have a "Member" web role and a "Guest" web role, each with different access.

- There are built-in web roles like "Authenticated Users" (users who sign in) and "Anonymous Users" (visitors who aren't signed in). The web role concept allows customization: you can create a new web role in the Portal Management app.

- Web roles tie in with table permissions, page permissions, and content access. For example, if a user is assigned the "Partner" web role, you can allow them to view certain pages, edit certain records, or access lists of data that other roles cannot.

Tip   Before you build your site flows, map out ahead of time what roles you'll need (e.g., Guest, Member, Editor, Admin) and what each role should access. It saves re-work later.

Important   Web roles are *not* the same as Dataverse security roles (which govern internal users). They are specific to the portal side (external site users) in Power Pages. Confusing the two can lead to access issues.

Web Files

Web files cover the static assets or downloadable content your site uses. Think of them as the "supporting files" used by your site for layout, script, styles, images, and documents.

- They might include CSS files (to define your site styling), JavaScript files (for client-side behavior), images, downloadable PDFs, or other assets.

- In Power Pages, you control where these files live and how they are served; they can be subject to permissions too (via page permissions or file permissions). For example, you can restrict a downloadable PDF only to users with a certain web role.

- Because performance is important, many sites will leverage a Content Delivery Network (CDN) for static web files so that assets load quickly for end users worldwide.

Tip   Use web files wisely, if you have many large images or heavy scripts, consider externalizing them or using optimized versions to keep your site fast.

Important   If you restrict access to web files (via permissions) make sure you're not accidentally blocking core CSS or JavaScript needed for your site UI, that can break the rendering or styling for all users.

Additional Tips for the Reader

- **Start with a Clear Purpose**: Before you build your site, define *who* your users will be and *what* they should do. That makes it easier to assign appropriate web roles and map data tables.

- **Design with Security in Mind**: Don't assume "public = everything." Use web roles and table permissions to restrict access to data.

- **Performance Matters**: Using the built-in CDN and optimizing web files helps deliver a better user experience.

- **Document Your Model**: Write down your site's structure (pages), data model (tables in Dataverse), roles (web roles), and files (web files). It will pay off when you scale or hand over the solution.

- **Test with Different Roles**: Sign in as different web roles (and as anonymous) to confirm that the site behaves as expected, for example, some pages visible, others hidden.

- **Don't Duplicate Work**: Many parts (tables, web roles, web files) can be reused across sites/environments. Think modularly.

Data Flow Overview Between Power Pages and Dataverse

When you build a site with Power Pages, one of the most critical things to understand is how the site and the data platform (Microsoft Dataverse) talk to each other, how information moves back and forth, what triggers updates, and where you need to pay attention in design and security. Figure 1-3 illustrates how Power Pages interacts with Dataverse. When a user performs an action on the site, the request securely travels to Dataverse for processing, triggering any required automation or workflows, and the processed data is then returned to the site for display.

How the Flow Works: Step by Step

1. **User Interaction on the Site**: A visitor lands on your site, maybe logs in, or remains anonymous. They click a link, fill out a form, view a list, or download a file.

2. **Site Request Reaches the Server**: That action triggers a request from the frontend site to the backend. The site is connected to Dataverse via a secure "server-to-server" channel, essentially the site's server contacts the Dataverse environment to retrieve or update data.

3. **Dataverse Receives the Request**: The request might be "Get me the list of support tickets for this user", or "Create a new record when this form is submitted". Dataverse processes that request, respects security permissions, executes business logic or workflows, and returns the result.

4. **Site Renders the Response**: The site receives data (e.g., the list of tickets) and displays it in the page the visitor sees. Or in the case of a form submission, once Dataverse has created or updated the record, the site may show a confirmation page or redirect the user accordingly.

5. **Optional Triggers and Automation**: Behind the scenes, when data changes in Dataverse it may trigger additional logic, for example, send an email alert, update another record, generate a workflow. Although the user just submitted a form on the site, the change may ripple elsewhere in your data model.

6. **Round-Trip and Caching**: Some assets (static files, images, scripts) may be cached through a CDN for performance, but the core data flow remains direct between the site server and Dataverse. The architecture is designed to keep data consistent and secure.

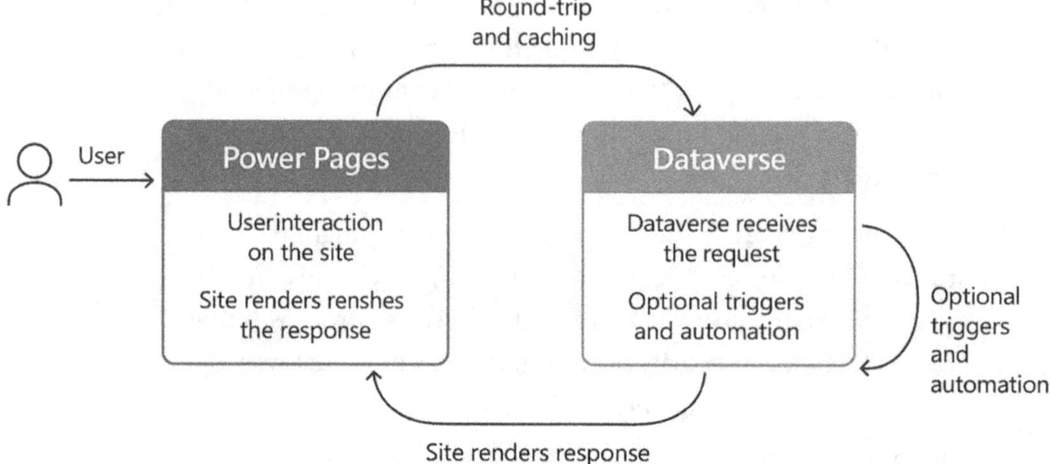

Figure 1-3. *Data Flow Between Power Pages and Dataverse*

Key Aspects to Keep in Mind

- **Authentication and Connection Channel**: The site doesn't act as a simple frontend doing blind reads and writes; it uses a secure connection to Dataverse. The system ensures that the site's server is authorized to talk to Dataverse.

- **Permission Enforcement**: Even though the user may fill a form or view a list, the system must enforce that only the right data is shown or edited, based on web roles and table permissions.

- **Data Consistency**: Because the site and the data live in tightly-coupled architecture, when you update in Dataverse the next time the site loads it should reflect that. Conversely, the site must structure its forms, lists, and pages to handle the real data correctly.

- **Performance and Latency**: Because each request potentially passes through Dataverse, you must design for efficiency. Large queries, unfiltered lists, heavy forms can slow things down. Caching static assets helps, but data retrieval still needs smart design.

- **Data Model Alignment**: The tables in Dataverse must match the expectations of the site. If your form expects "Customer Status" values, you must ensure your table holds them. If your list shows related data (like "Orders for this Customer"), you must set up the relationships.

- **Automation and Logic Triggered by the Site**: When your site leads to data changes, there may be workflows, business rules, or triggers defined in Dataverse. These can create additional records, send alerts, or modify data; you should know how your site actions might set off this chain.

Core Capabilities and Benefits

The goal of Power Pages is to lower the barrier to building web experiences, while still giving room for pro-developer depth when needed. In today's digital world, organizations want to deliver professional websites quickly, without depending entirely on specialized web developers or long development cycles. Power Pages meets this need by combining **low-code tools**, **AI-driven assistance**, and **built-in responsive design** into a single, unified platform.

With Power Pages, anyone from a business analyst to a professional developer can create dynamic, secure, and data-connected websites. Its **low-code design environment** allows makers to visually compose pages, add data components, and style their site through simple configuration rather than complex coding. This accelerates development while maintaining professional quality.

To make things even faster, **AI-assisted building** introduces intelligent suggestions and automation into the design process. Makers can describe what they want to create, and Power Pages automatically generates forms, layouts, and text content. This feature reduces the time spent on repetitive tasks and empowers users who may not have design or technical expertise.

Finally, **responsive design** ensures that every site you build adapts seamlessly across devices, whether it's a mobile phone, tablet, or desktop. Power Pages automatically adjusts layouts and visual elements to deliver an optimal experience for every screen size, saving you from the manual effort of designing separate versions for each device.

Together, these three capabilities make Power Pages a powerful yet approachable platform, one that blends simplicity and flexibility, enabling organizations to build modern, data-rich websites faster than ever before.

Low-Code Development, AI-Assisted Building, Responsive Design

With Power Pages, you don't need to be a full-time web developer to create a professional, data-connected website. The design studio provides visual tools: drag-and-drop page components, theming workspaces, templates that you can modify. This means you can launch a website faster, utilize prebuilt pieces, and focus on the business value rather than on writing all the HTML, CSS, JavaScript from scratch.

Benefits are shorter time-to-market, lower reliance on specialized coding skills, more possibilities for IT-and-business-team collaboration.

Even though it's low-code, you'll still benefit from good planning: data models, roles, and user experience must be thought through; the visual tools don't replace good architecture.

AI-Assisted Building

Power Pages has started to embed AI capabilities (such as Copilot-style assistance) to help with content generation, design suggestions, and building forms/pages more quickly. For example, you might describe what you need and the tool can provide a starting design or generate text content, thereby accelerating the build process and reducing repetitive work.

Makes site creation faster, helps non-technical makers get started, reduces the burden of "blank page" syndrome.

AI assistance is a help, not a substitute for governance and clarity. Generated content still needs review (for brand tone, accuracy, accessibility, performance). Don't skip those checks.

Responsive Design

Modern websites must look and work well on desktops, tablets, phones. Power Pages handles this by providing responsive templates and previews so you design once and the site adapts across device types. This means fewer device-specific tweaks, and a better experience for users on any device.

A responsive design in Power Apps provides broader reach across devices (mobile, tablet, and laptop), ensures consistent branding and layout, and reduces device-specific maintenance efforts. Responsive design doesn't absolve you from testing on actual devices or ensuring performance (e.g., large images, heavy scripts can still slow down mobile). Always test and optimize for performance and usability on the full range of devices your users might use.

Consolidated Summary

By combining low-code development, AI-assisted building, and responsive design, Power Pages empowers both business makers and developers to deliver websites faster, with less effort, and for more devices, while still maintaining the ability to dive deep when required.

Tip   If you're just starting, pick a template and use the AI features to generate the initial draft of a site page (layout + content). Then iterate: refine the form, optimize for mobile, and map to your data model.

Important   Don't assume "low-code" means "no planning." Good design, data structure, security and performance considerations still apply. Treat this like any serious web project.

Integration with Other Power Platform Tools

Power Pages doesn't exist in isolation, it's part of the larger **Microsoft Power Platform ecosystem**, which includes Power Apps, Power Automate, Power BI, and Copilot Studio. This tight integration makes Power Pages more than just a website builder; it becomes a bridge that connects people, processes, and data within your organization. Through these connections, your site can not only display information but also trigger actions, visualize insights, and interact intelligently with users.

Power Apps Integration

Power Pages and Power Apps share the same data foundation, Microsoft Dataverse. This means any table, form, or record created in Power Apps can be easily displayed or updated through a Power Pages site.

For example, if your internal team uses a Power App to manage service requests, you can extend the same data externally through Power Pages, allowing customers or partners to log requests, track progress, or update details directly through a secure web interface.

This seamless connection removes the need for data duplication and ensures everyone interacts with the same, up-to-date information.

Power Automate Integration

With **Power Automate**, actions on your Power Pages site can trigger automated workflows that streamline your business processes. When a user submits a form, creates a record, or updates information, a flow can automatically send notifications, update related data, or generate approvals in the background.

For instance, submitting a "Contact Us" form on your site could start a workflow that sends an email confirmation to the user, assigns a follow-up task in Microsoft Teams, and records the interaction in your CRM system, all without manual intervention.

This integration adds intelligence and efficiency to your website, turning it into an active participant in your organizational workflow.

Power BI Integration

Power BI brings **interactive data visualization** to your Power Pages site. You can embed dashboards or individual reports directly into your web pages, allowing users to view data insights in real time. For internal users, these dashboards can provide performance metrics, sales data, or service analytics. For external users, you can present curated, role-based views that inform and engage without exposing sensitive details.

Embedding Power BI content transforms a Power Pages site from a static web portal into a dynamic data experience where users don't just view content, they understand and act on it.

Copilot Studio and AI Integration

Power Pages can also integrate with **Copilot Studio** to create AI-powered chatbots and guided experiences. You can embed a Copilot directly into your website to help users navigate pages, answer questions, or perform actions such as checking order status or submitting feedback.

These AI-driven assistants enhance accessibility, improve response times, and provide personalized interactions, all while working with the same Dataverse data that powers your site.

Tip   When designing your Power Pages solution, think beyond the website itself. Plan how Power Apps, Power Automate, Power BI, and Copilot Studio can each play a role in your user journey. A single site can easily become a unified entry point for actions, insights, and automation across the entire Power Platform.

Important   While integration adds immense value, it also introduces complexity. Always define clear ownership and governance, who manages the data, who maintains the flows, and who secures the analytics. Proper coordination ensures smooth operation and prevents performance or security issues across connected environments.

Environment Setup

Before building your first Power Pages site, it is essential to prepare the right environment and ensure that all required platform components are correctly configured. Power Pages operates on top of Microsoft Dataverse and the broader Power Platform ecosystem, so a proper setup ensures that your site is secure, scalable, and ready for development. This process begins with understanding the licensing options and prerequisites needed to enable Power Pages features within your tenant. Once the requirements are in place, you will create either a trial environment or a dedicated developer environment, both of which offer a safe, isolated space to explore the platform and begin building without impacting production data. As a final step, Dataverse must be provisioned and configured because it serves as the foundational data layer for your pages, forms, and authentication workflows. By completing this foundational setup, you prepare a stable and governed environment that supports everything you will build throughout the rest of this book.

Licensing and Prerequisites

To start building applications with Power Pages, the first step is to ensure your tenant has the appropriate licensing and that your environment meets baseline prerequisites. Power Pages is now licensed separately under the Power Platform licensing model; it no longer requires a separate "portal-add-on" license as was the case with the older portals offering. Table 1-2 shows how to choose the right Power Pages model.

License Types and How They Work

Power Pages licensing is based on the number of users of your website, rather than a fixed seat-based license. There are two broad licensing approaches: capacity-based subscription and pay-as-you-go.

- **Authenticated Users Per Website**: For users who log in (using an identity provider) to your Power Pages website. Licenses are sold in "capacity packs" (e.g., 100 authenticated users per pack/month in a subscription model).

- **Anonymous Users Per Website**: For users who browse the website without logging in (i.e., public/guest access). Anonymous-user capacity packs typically support 500 anonymous users per pack/month.

You choose the capacity based on expected usage. If your site usage is predictable and stable, a capacity-based subscription makes sense. If usage varies (for example, bursts of traffic), the pay-as-you-go model may be more cost-effective.

Importantly, there is **no longer a separate "base license" prerequisite** (as was required in older portal licensing models). Power Pages stands alone, you can license it directly.

Also note: if your organization already uses a premium Power Platform license (e.g., Power Apps "per user" or a Dynamics 365 Enterprise license), these may include usage rights for Power Pages, which means those licensed users may not always count toward your capacity-pack usage meters.

Storage and Capacity Entitlements

When you purchase capacity packs for Power Pages, they also come with additional storage capacity allocated to your environment (via Microsoft Dataverse). For example:

- Authenticated user capacity packs include **2 GB database capacity + 16 GB file capacity** (per pack) allocated at the tenant level.

- Anonymous user capacity packs contribute more modest storage entitlements (e.g., 0.5 GB database + 4 GB file capacity).

If you choose a pay-as-you-go model instead of subscription, initial storage entitlement is more modest (e.g., a one-time allocation of around 1 GB database and 1 GB file capacity when environment is created under PAYG).

System and Tenant Prerequisites

Before you begin using Power Pages (designing, building, or publishing a site), ensure the following:

- Your environment must support Dataverse (as Power Pages data, authentication, and content storage rely on Dataverse).

- To create or administer a site, you need adequate permissions, for example, the roles of "Power Platform administrator" or "Dynamics 365 administrator" (or similar), or global/billing admin privileges if managing licensing.

- Your browsers and operating system must meet the supported platform requirements for Power Pages Design Studio and runtime. For example, supported browsers are recent versions of Chrome, Edge, Firefox, or Safari (for site visitors).

- Network configuration must allow access to the set of Microsoft and Power Platform domains required for authentication, site rendering, storage, and backend services.

Table 1-2. *Choosing the Right Power Pages Licensing Model*

Scenario	Best Licensing Option	Why This Option Fits	Ideal For
You are learning, experimenting, or building a prototype	**Developer/Trial Environment**	Free, safe for testing; full Power Pages capability without impact on production	Students, trainers, early exploration, demos
Your website traffic is steady and predictable each month	**Subscription (Capacity-Based)**	Fixed monthly packs for authenticated and anonymous users; predictable budgeting	Corporate portals, partner portals, ongoing public sites
Your site traffic varies or is seasonal	**Pay-as-You-Go (Azure Metered)**	Pay only for actual authenticated logins and unique visitors; cost scales with usage	Event sites, campaigns, low-traffic portals, unpredictable workloads
You already have Power Apps or Dynamics licenses for internal staff	**Included Usage Rights**	No additional cost for internal authenticated users; uses existing entitlements	Intranet portals, employee self-service pages
You need a low-risk setup for development before production	**Sandbox Environment with Power Pages Enabled**	Allows configuration, testing integrations, and validating security before go-live	Developers, solution architects, QA teams

Creating a Trial or Developer Environment

Before building your first Power Pages site, you need an environment where Power Pages and Dataverse are enabled. Microsoft provides two primary options: a **trial environment** and a **developer environment**, each designed to help you explore the platform without impacting production systems. Both allow you to experiment freely with site creation, Copilot, Dataverse tables, security configuration, and integrations. Table 1-3 shows the requirements to choose trial and developer environments.

Using a Trial Environment

A **trial environment** is the fastest way to get started with Power Pages. It is time-limited but provides full functionality, making it ideal for short-term evaluation or hands-on exercises.

Key Characteristics:

- Typically, valid for **30 days**, with an option to extend depending on your tenant

- Includes **Dataverse**, Power Pages, Power Apps, and Power Automate

- Allows external user setup, form creation, table permissions, and site deployment for testing

- Designed for quick onboarding, proofs of concept, and training scenarios

How to Create a Trial Environment:

1. Navigate to **Power Pages** home (`https://make.powerpages.microsoft.com`).

2. Select **Try Power Pages** or **Get Started**, depending on your region and tenant experience.

3. Sign in with your work or school account; Microsoft automatically provisions a trial instance.

4. Once created, the environment appears in the environment selector, ready to host your first site.

Trial environments are disposable by design, perfect for learning, workshops, or working through the chapters of this book.

Using the Developer Environment (Power Apps Developer Plan)

For readers who prefer a long-term, free environment, Microsoft offers the **Power Apps Developer Plan**. This provides a persistent, fully functional Dataverse environment that supports Power Pages development.

Key Characteristics:

- Entirely **free for personal use** (not for production deployment)

- Includes **Dataverse**, solution management, Power Pages, Power Apps, and Power Automate

- Ideal for building complete sample portals, testing enterprise scenarios, and practicing ALM (Application Lifecycle Management)

- Not accessible to external users in production mode, but fully functional for internal development and training

How to Create a Developer Environment:

1. Register for the **Power Apps Developer Plan** by signing in at `https://powerapps.microsoft.com/developerplan`.

2. After sign-up, open the **Power Platform Admin Center**.

3. A new environment named *Developer* (or similar) will automatically appear in your tenant.

4. Ensure that **Dataverse is provisioned**, if not, the platform will prompt you to create it.

5. Enable **Power Pages** within the environment and begin building your site.

Developer environments are the best option for continuous learning, book exercises, and testing advanced features like Liquid templates, web API integration, and code components.

Table 1-3. *Choosing Between Trial and Developer Environments*

Requirement	Best Option
Short-term evaluation, workshop, or guided learning	**Trial Environment**
Long-term practice, repeated experimentation, solution development	**Developer Environment**
Need external user login simulation	**Trial Environment**
Need unlimited learning environment with Dataverse	**Developer Environment**

Setting Up Dataverse

Microsoft Dataverse is the foundational data platform that powers every Power Pages site. It stores the tables, relationships, forms, lists, and security configuration that your site will use. Because Power Pages is tightly integrated with Dataverse, setting it up correctly is a critical step before creating pages or exposing data to external users. Once Dataverse is provisioned in your environment, the platform automatically enables the structures and services required for building secure, data-driven websites.

Provisioning Dataverse

In many environments, such as newly created trial or developer environments, Dataverse is provisioned automatically. However, if it is not yet installed, the Power Platform Admin Center will prompt you to create it.

To Provision Dataverse:

1. Open the **Power Platform Admin Center** (`https://admin.powerplatform.microsoft.com`).

2. Select your environment (trial, developer, or sandbox).

3. If Dataverse is not enabled, you will see an option to **Create a database**.

4. Choose your region and language settings.

5. Confirm and allow the platform to complete provisioning.

Provisioning Dataverse may take several minutes, as the system creates essential tables, the security model, search services, and the metadata infrastructure required for Power Pages.

Understanding Dataverse Structures for Power Pages

Once Dataverse is active, Power Pages gains immediate access to

- **Standard tables** such as Contact, Account, and Web Roles

- **Custom tables** you create to support portal functionality

- **Supporting metadata** including forms, views, choices, and relationships

- **Security layers** such as table permissions, authentication mappings, and web roles

These elements form the backbone of your site. For example:

- **Tables** store the data displayed on your website.

- **Forms** and **views** determine how users interact with data.

- **Table permissions** and **web roles** define what each external user can see or edit.

Understanding how Dataverse organizes data will help you configure forms, lists, authentication, and advanced features covered later in the book.

Preparing Dataverse for Development

Before building your first site, it is recommended to set up a minimal structure in Dataverse:

- Create required **custom tables** to store business data.

- Review **standard tables**, such as Contact, for external identity mapping.

- Configure **columns**, **relationships**, and **choice fields** based on your portal scenario.

- Set up **solutions** (optional but recommended) to manage components cleanly, especially if you plan to migrate your site later.

Creating this foundation ensures consistency and makes later development, such as building multistep forms or using Code Components, much easier to manage.

Verifying Dataverse Integration with Power Pages

After Dataverse is set up, verify that Power Pages can access it:

- Open **Power Pages Design Studio** and create a test site.

- Navigate to the **Data workspace** and confirm you can see tables and forms.

- Try adding a **list** or **form** to a page to confirm data connectivity.

- Confirm that the **Contacts** table is visible, as it is required for authenticated users.

If all these elements appear, your environment is fully ready for development.

Important   Power Pages **cannot function without Dataverse**, so ensure the environment's Dataverse database is fully provisioned before creating your site.

Tip   When working in a trial or developer environment, create your Dataverse tables and Power Pages components inside a solution so you can easily move or version them later.

Exploring the Power Pages Interface

Before you start building pages, forms, and data-driven components, it's important to become familiar with the Power Pages interface. The interface is designed to be intuitive for beginners while still offering depth for advanced users. Through a single, unified experience, you can create sites, design pages, style layouts, manage data integration, and configure security, all without switching between multiple tools.

Power Pages provides a modern **Design Studio** experience that brings together visual page editing, theming, data configuration, and setup options in one place. Whether you are a business user exploring low-code development or a professional developer preparing for advanced customization, understanding this interface will help you work more efficiently as you progress through the book.

To get hands-on experience while following along with the examples in this chapter, Microsoft offers a **30-day free trial** for Power Pages. This trial allows you to explore the full interface, create a site, and experiment with key features such as Dataverse integration, authentication, and page design, without impacting any production environment.

You are encouraged to activate the free trial and explore the interface as you read through the next sections of this chapter.

Try Power Pages Free for 30 Days:

```
https://www.microsoft.com/en-us/power-platform/try-free?tsapp=powerpages
```

Figure 1-4 shows the **Microsoft Power Pages 30-day free trial registration screen**, where users can begin exploring Power Pages without any upfront cost. This page highlights the no-code approach to building modern business websites and outlines key capabilities such as using professionally designed templates, customizing branding elements like colors and fonts, adding sections and components, and connecting data through Microsoft Dataverse. On the right side of the screen, users are prompted to enter their email address and accept the Microsoft Online Subscription Agreement to start the free trial, making this the first step in accessing the Power Pages Design Studio and environment setup.

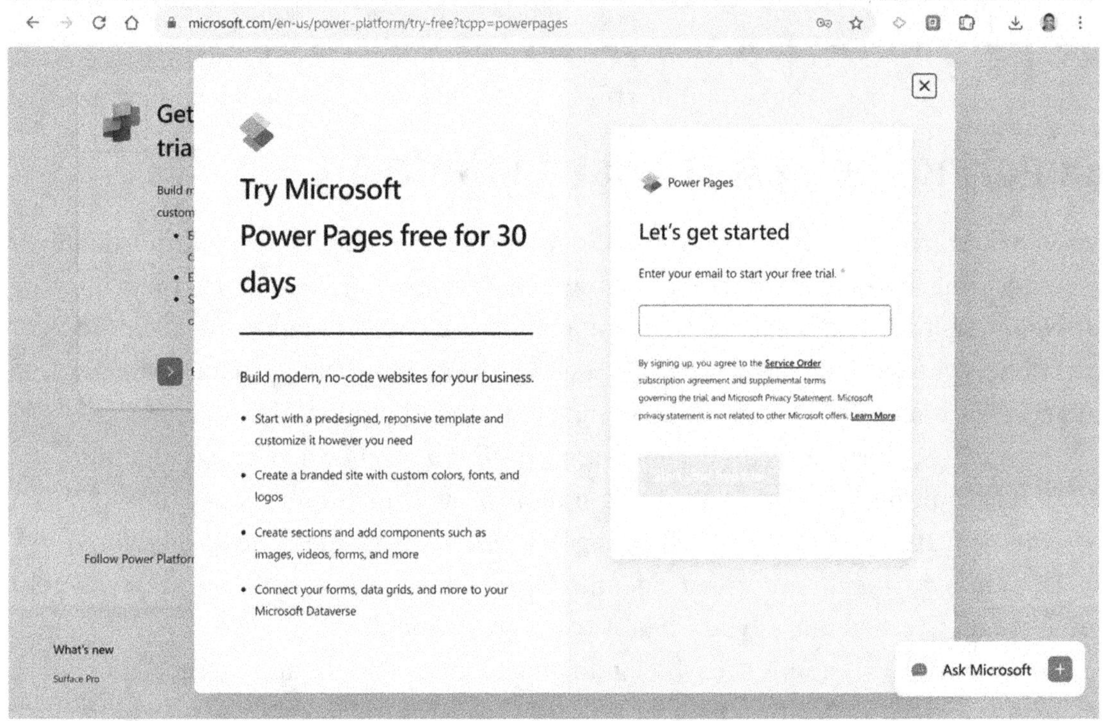

Figure 1-4. *Power Pages 30-Day Free Trial Sign-Up Screen*

Figure 1-5 illustrates the **user information collection screen** displayed after initiating the Power Pages free trial. This step gathers essential details such as job title, country or region, and phone number to complete the trial setup. The form also includes consent options related to receiving information from Microsoft and its partners, ensuring compliance with privacy and communication preferences. This screen represents an important onboarding step, as it helps Microsoft personalize the trial experience and enables users to proceed toward accessing the Power Pages environment and design studio.

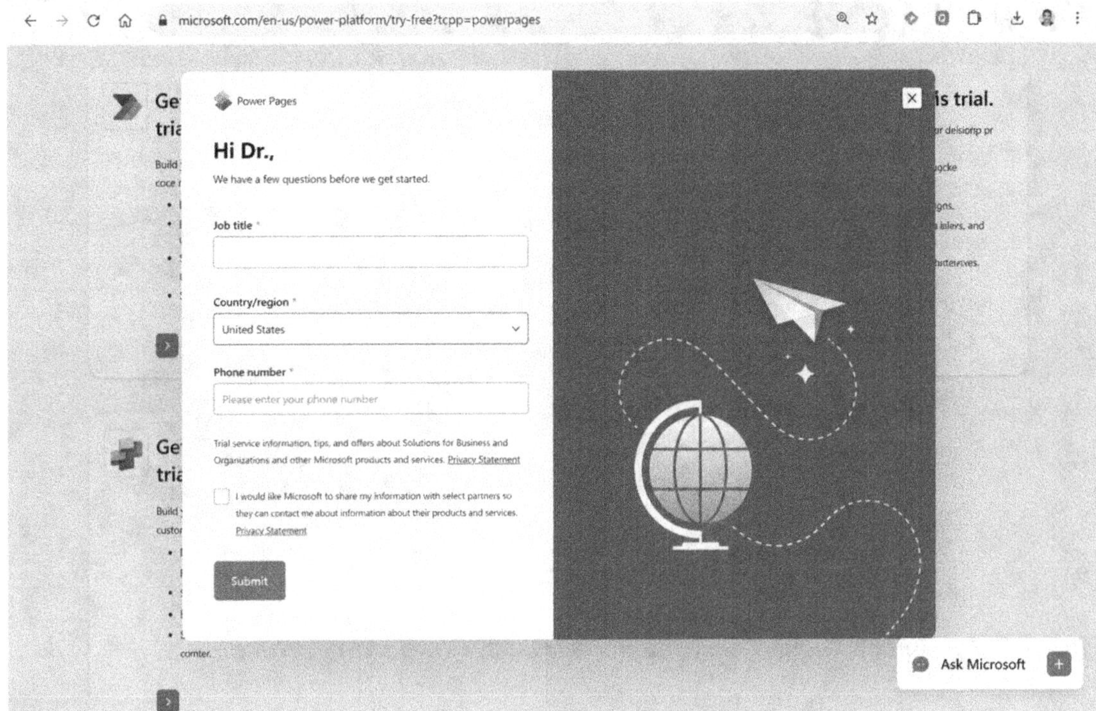

Figure 1-5. *Power Pages Trial User Information Form*

Figure 1-6 displays the **Power Pages welcome screen** shown after successfully completing the trial registration and initial setup. This screen introduces users to Power Pages and highlights the inclusion of **Copilot**, the generative AI feature that assists in creating websites by describing requirements in natural language. The "Get started" option initiates a guided onboarding process, where Power Pages asks a few questions to tailor the site-building experience. This screen marks the transition from account setup to actively building and customizing a Power Pages website within the selected environment. Figure 1-7 illustrates the **industry selection step** in the Power Pages onboarding process, where users are asked to specify the type of industry for which they are creating a website. The screen presents predefined options such as Education, Finance, Government, Healthcare, Manufacturing, Nonprofit, Transportation, and Other. Selecting an industry helps Power Pages personalize the in-product experience, templates, and recommendations based on the user's domain and expertise. This step enables a more tailored site-building journey and ensures that the generated website aligns closely with industry-specific needs and use cases.

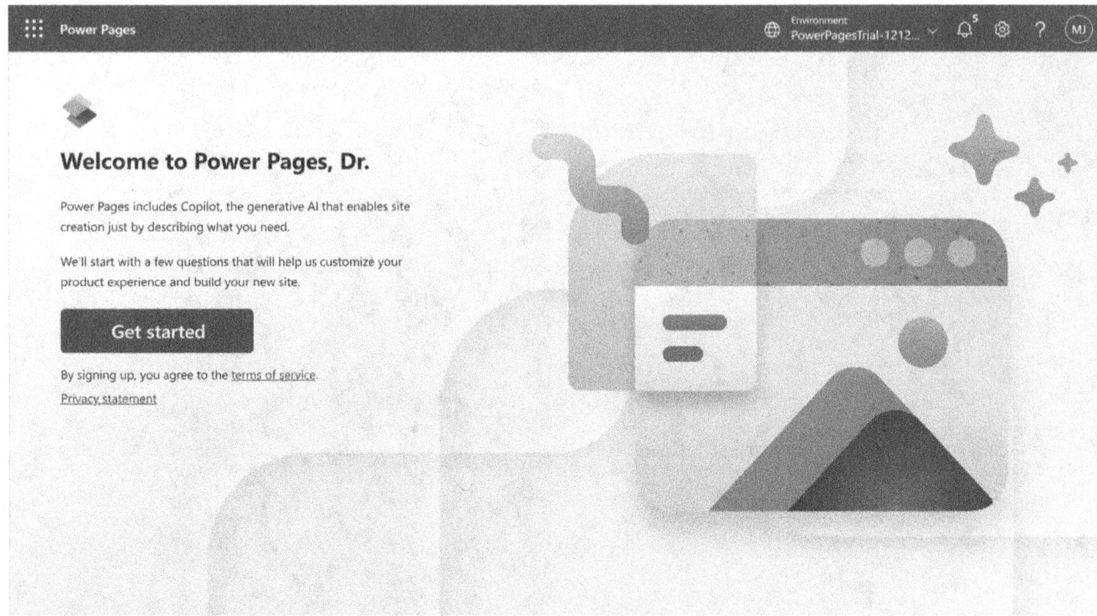

Figure 1-6. *Power Pages Welcome Screen with Copilot Introduction*

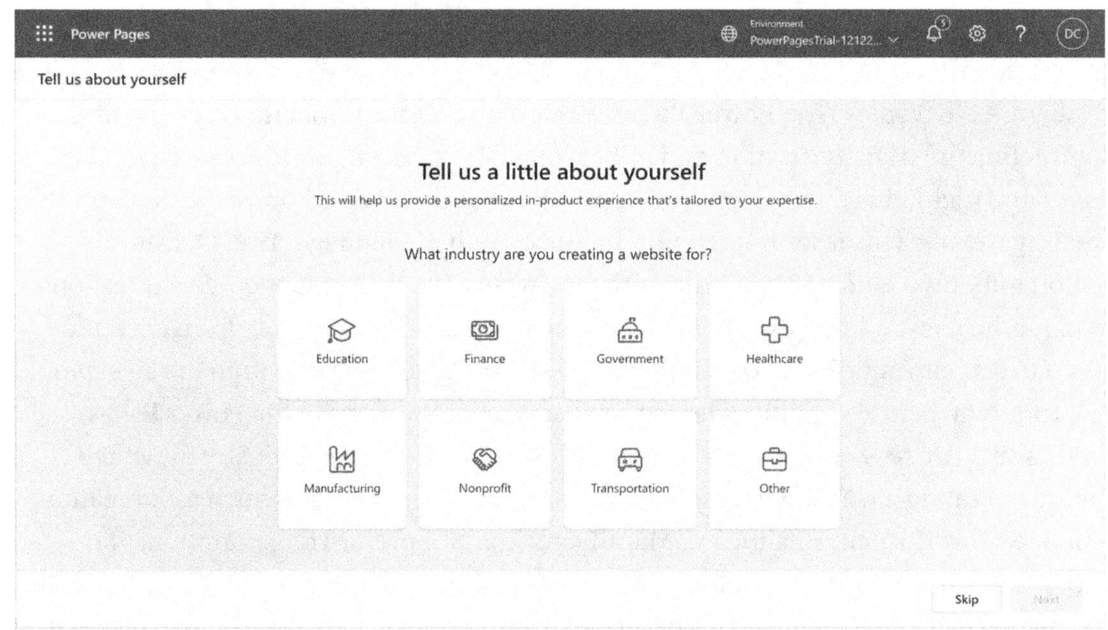

Figure 1-7. *Industry Selection Screen During Power Pages Onboarding (Optional Step)*

Figure 1-8 shows the **Copilot-assisted site creation screen** in Power Pages, where users are guided to describe the website they want to build using generative AI. The screen presents suggested use cases such as Event Registration and Management, Feedback and Survey Collection, Appointment Scheduling and Tracking, and Membership Registration and Management.

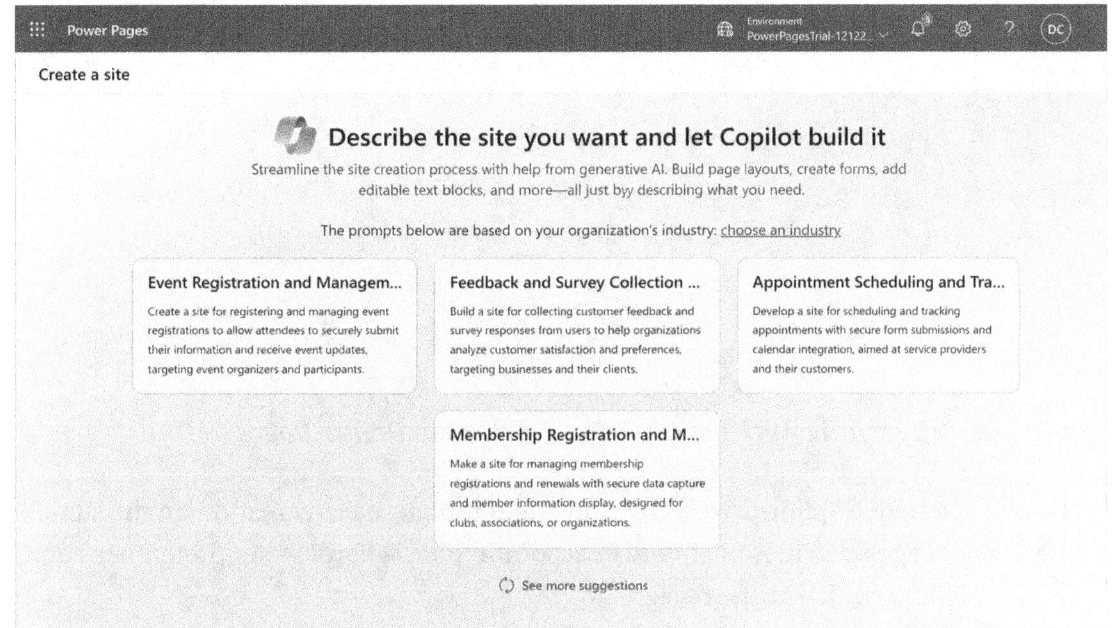

Figure 1-8. *Creating a Website Using Copilot with Suggested Use Cases*

These suggestions act as starting points, helping users quickly select a scenario or refine their requirements so that Copilot can automatically generate page layouts, forms, and content blocks. This step simplifies the website creation process by allowing users to build a functional site by describing their needs rather than designing everything from scratch.

Figure 1-9 illustrates the **alternative approach to creating a website in Power Pages**, presented on the same page shown in Figure 1-8. In addition to using Copilot to describe requirements in natural language, this section highlights the option to **start with a template** by selecting from a gallery of prebuilt site templates. This option is useful for users who prefer a structured starting point rather than AI-assisted generation.

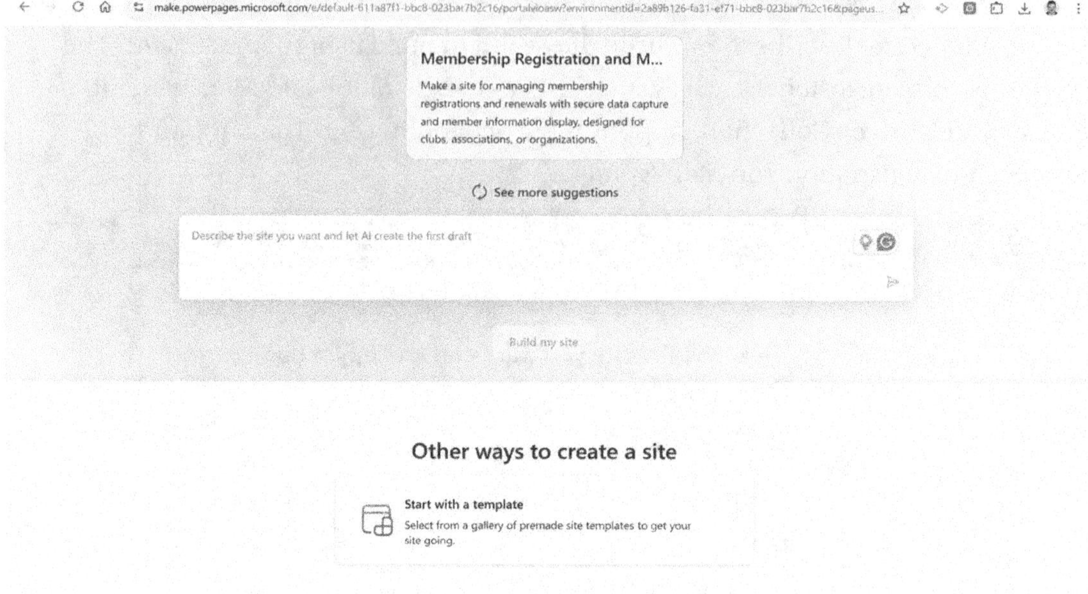

Figure 1-9. *Alternative Website Creation Options in Power Pages*

By offering both Copilot-driven creation and template-based creation on the same screen, Power Pages provides flexibility to accommodate different user preferences and levels of familiarity with website design.

Figure 1-10 shows the **template selection screen** in Power Pages, where users choose a starting template based on the functionality required for their website. The screen categorizes templates into different groups such as Starter layouts, Scheduling, Application submission, Registration, Dynamics 365, and FAQ, allowing users to quickly filter and identify suitable designs.

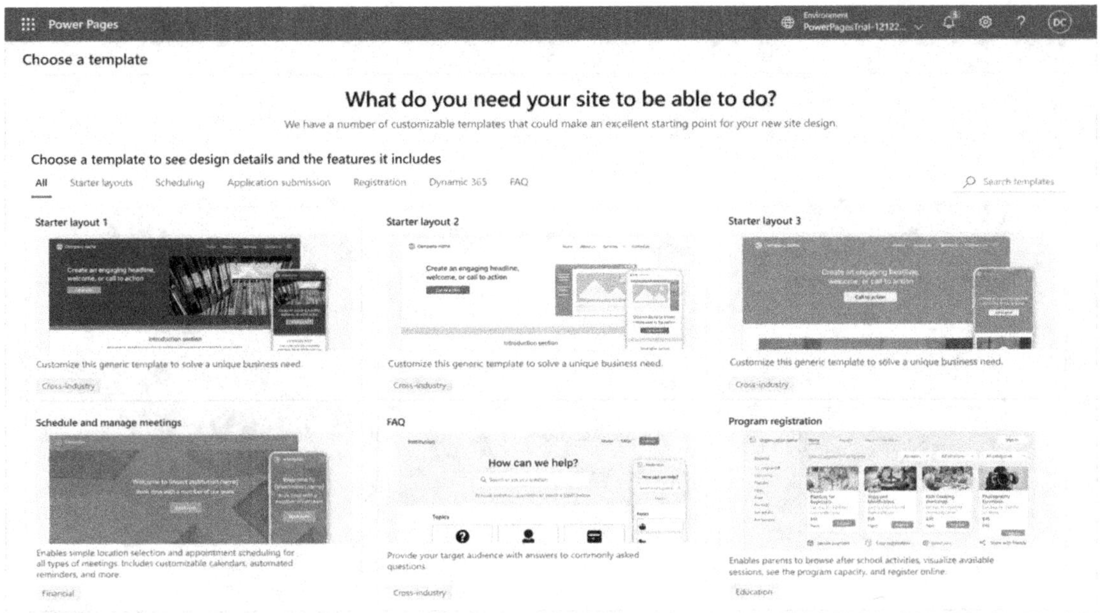

Figure 1-10. *Template Selection Screen in Power Pages*

Each template preview highlights the layout and features included, enabling users to select a template that can be customized further to meet specific business requirements. This step provides a structured and guided approach to website creation for users who prefer starting with predefined designs rather than generating a site using Copilot.

Figure 1-11 illustrates the **template preview and selection option** within the Power Pages template gallery. When a user hovers over or selects a template, options such as **Preview template** and **choose this template** become available, allowing users to review the design and features before making a selection. This step enables informed decision-making by giving users a visual understanding of the layout and structure of the template, ensuring that the chosen template aligns with the website's intended purpose and customization requirements before proceeding to the next stage of site creation.

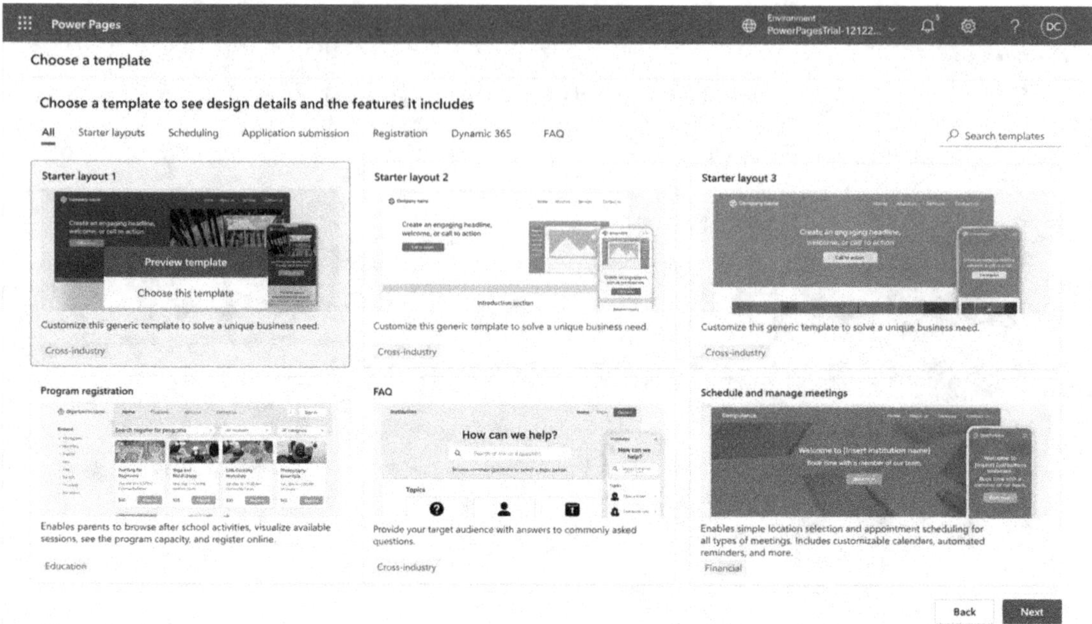

Figure 1-11. *Previewing and Selecting a Starter Template in Power Pages*

Figure 1-12 shows the **site details configuration screen** in Power Pages, where users provide essential information to initialize their new website. This step requires entering a site name and creating a unique web address that will be used as the site's URL under the Power Pages domain.

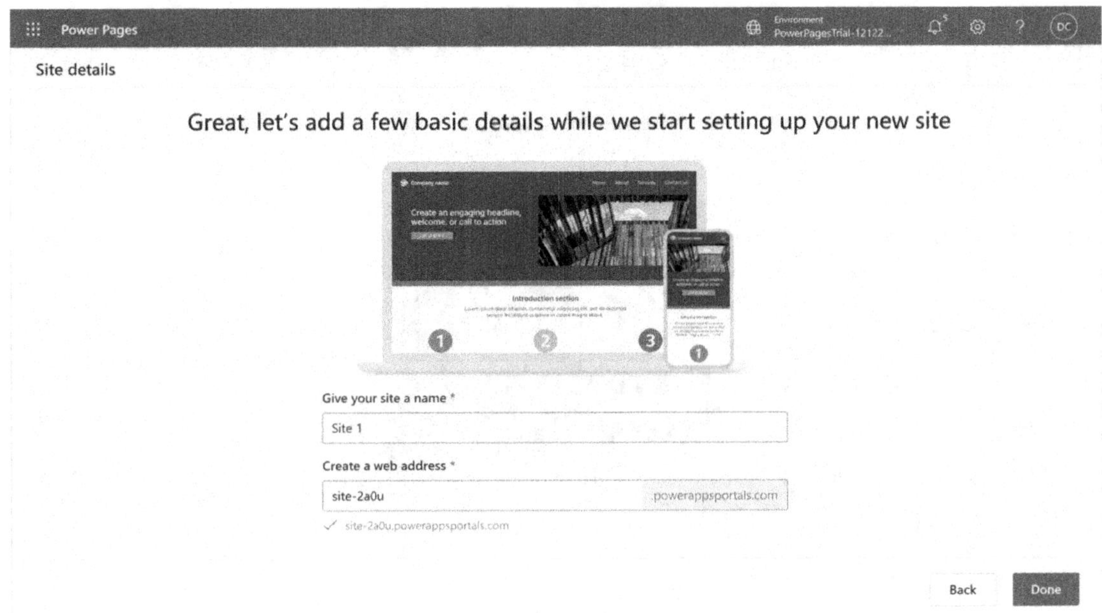

Figure 1-12. *Entering Basic Site Details in Power Pages*

These basic details are used to provision the site and make it accessible once setup is complete. Completing this step finalizes the initial configuration and allows Power Pages to proceed with creating the website based on the selected template and settings.

Figure 1-13 depicts the **site provisioning screen** displayed while Power Pages is setting up the new website and associated environment. This screen informs the user that the site creation process is in progress and may take a few minutes to complete. During this phase, Power Pages provisions the required resources, applies the selected template, and prepares the home page for access. Once the setup is finished, users are automatically redirected to the site's home page to begin exploring and customizing their newly created Power Pages website.

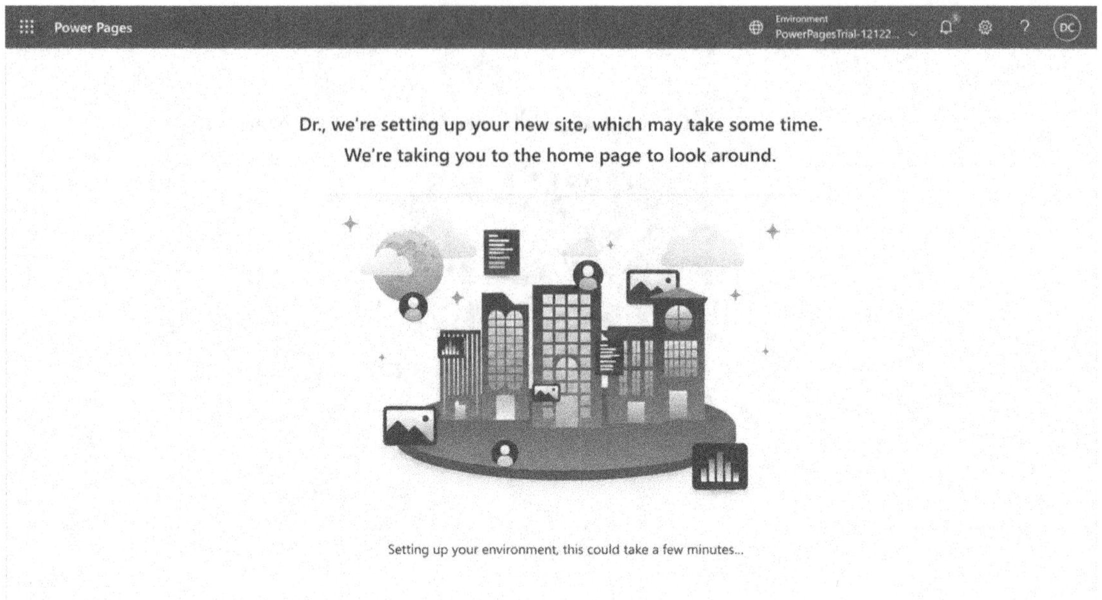

Figure 1-13. *Site Provisioning and Environment Setup in Power Pages*

Design Studio Overview

The **Power Pages Design Studio** provides an intuitive, low-code environment that
enables makers to build, customize, and manage rich, data-driven business websites
with ease. It offers a visual editing experience that allows you to design pages, configure
layouts, and connect data, all without writing a single line of code.

Figure 1-14 shows the **Power Pages Design Studio interface** after the site has been
successfully created. The screen displays the page-editing canvas in the center, the
Pages navigation pane on the left for managing site structure, and the **Copilot panel**
on the right that assists with page design, data forms, and answering questions. Users
can visually edit page content, add sections and components, and navigate between
pages without writing code, while also having the option to switch to code view if
required. This interface serves as the primary workspace for designing, customizing, and
managing Power Pages websites efficiently.

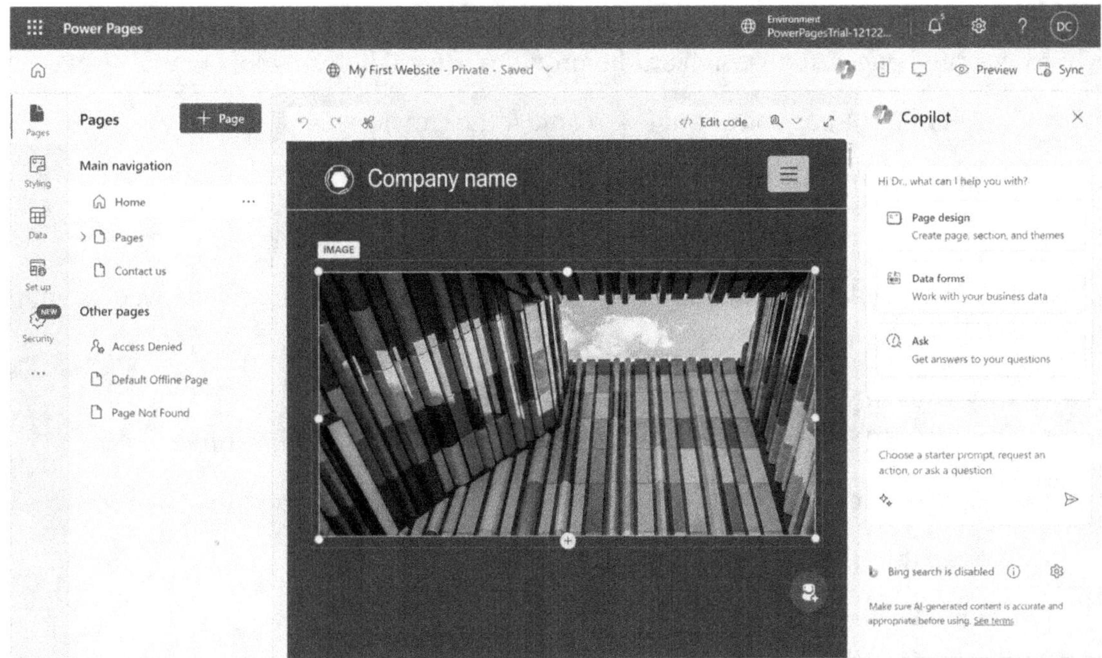

Figure 1-14. *Power Pages Design Studio with Copilot Panel*

Important   To edit a site using the Design Studio, you must be assigned the appropriate roles and permissions within the same Microsoft Dataverse environment where the site is hosted.

Design Studio Workspaces

The Design Studio is organized into four core **workspaces**, each tailored to a specific task:

- **Pages**: Create and manage pages, navigation, and layout

- **Styling**: Apply themes, branding, and visual styles

- **Data**: Configure data sources, forms, and lists

- **Setup**: Manage site settings, authentication, and integrations

This workspace-based approach helps you stay focused and work efficiently as you design your site.

Page Editing Options

While designing pages, the Design Studio provides several helpful tools:

- **Zoom in (+)** or **zoom out (–)** to adjust the canvas view

- **Reset zoom** to return to the default page size

- **Switch to code editor** when you need advanced customization

These options allow you to fine-tune your design and quickly switch between visual and code-based editing.

Previewing Your Site

Once you have made changes, you can preview your site before publishing:

- Use **Preview → Desktop** to open the site in a new browser tab

- Scan the **QR code** to preview the site on a mobile device

- Email a preview link to view the site on mobile

Previewing ensures that your site looks and behaves as expected across devices.

Accessing the Portal Management App and Syncing Changes

For advanced configurations not available in the Design Studio, such as detailed metadata management or legacy portal settings, you can access the **Portal Management app**:

1. Select the **ellipsis (···)** icon from the left-hand navigation menu.

2. Choose **Portal Management** from the additional options.

After making changes in the Portal Management app, select **Sync** in the upper-right corner of the Design Studio to ensure that all updates are reflected in the visual editor.

Understanding Security Basics

Security is the foundation of every Power Pages implementation. Because Power Pages exposes Dataverse data to external audiences, it uses a layered security model that combines authentication, authorization, and data-access policies. At an introductory level, two key areas must be understood: **how users authenticate** into your site and **how permissions control what they can do once authenticated**.

Authentication Types (Azure AD, Local, External IDPs)

Power Pages supports multiple authentication methods so organizations can allow external users to sign in using the identity systems they already use. Authentication defines **who** the user is before determining **what** they can access. Table 1-4 provides a consolidated comparison of all authentication methods supported in Power Pages, outlining how users sign in, the scenarios each method is best suited for, and the key benefits and considerations to keep in mind when configuring secure access for your site.

Azure Active Directory (Microsoft Entra ID)

Azure AD (now Microsoft Entra ID) is commonly used when your portal needs secure sign-in for employees, partners, or B2B/B2C users. It supports

- Single sign-on

- Conditional Access

- Multi-factor authentication

- B2B collaboration with guest accounts

This is the most secure and enterprise-friendly option for regulated industries or internal/external partner access scenarios.

Local Authentication (Username + Password)

Local authentication allows users to create a **local portal account** with an email address and password.

It is useful for

- Public-facing sites with open registration

- Lightweight onboarding

- Users who do not have organizational identities

Local accounts are stored in Dataverse as Contacts mapped to their identity provider record.

However, it is less secure than enterprise identity providers, so Microsoft recommends using external identity providers for most production scenarios.

External Identity Providers (IDPs)

Power Pages can connect with standards-based identity providers such as

- **Azure AD B2C**

- **Google**

- **Facebook**

- **LinkedIn**

- **Microsoft Account**

- Any provider that supports **OpenID Connect** or **SAML 2.0**

This enables flexible authentication for large public audiences without needing to manage user credentials. Each identity provider maps authenticated users to **Contact records** in Dataverse.

Anonymous Access (Optional)

Sites can allow anonymous browsing of selected pages.

Anonymous access is often enabled for

- Marketing content

- Public information pages

- General information portals

However, anonymous users cannot submit forms or access personalized data unless explicitly configured using secure table permissions.

Web Roles and Table Permissions (Intro Level)

Once a user signs in, Power Pages uses **web roles** and **table permissions** to determine what they can see or do within the site. This mapping forms the core of the authorization model.

Web Roles (Site-Level Permissions)

A web role defines **what level of access** a user has inside the portal.

Examples of common built-in roles include

- **Administrators**: Full control over site content

- **Authenticated Users**: General registered users

- **Anonymous Users**: Public visitors

A user can have multiple web roles assigned to their Dataverse Contact record. Web roles determine whether a user can access components such as

- Specific pages

- Forms

- Lists

- Admin features

- Custom functionality

Web roles are the bridge between user identity and the permissions you want to enforce within Power Pages.

Table Permissions (Dataverse Access Control)

Table permissions determine **what Dataverse data** a user can access once authenticated.

Each permission rule includes

- The **table** (e.g., Contact, Case, Custom table)

- The **scope** of access (Global, Contact, Account, Parent, Self)

- The **rights** (Read, Write, Create, Delete, Append, Append To)

For example:

- *Authenticated users can view only the records they created.*

- *Partner users can view records linked to their account.*

- *Administrators can view or manage all records.*

Permissions are evaluated **on top of** web roles.
This means:

- A page may be visible, but data will not load unless table permissions allow access.

- Even with authentication, users cannot bypass Dataverse security layers.

Table 1-4. *Authentication Types Supported in Power Pages*

Authentication Type	How Users Sign In	Best For	Key Benefits	Considerations
Azure AD/ Microsoft Entra ID (B2B/B2C)	Using organizational or guest accounts	Employee portals, partner portals, enterprise apps	– Enterprise-grade security – Conditional Access, MFA – Supports B2B collaboration	Requires Azure setup; managed identities only
External Identity Providers (OIDC/ SAML)	Using accounts like Google, LinkedIn, Facebook, or any OpenID/SAML provider	Public sites, wide audience portals, customer engagement	– Familiar logins for users – No password management – Easy onboarding	Must configure provider details (client ID, secret, redirect URLs)
Local Authentication (Email + Password)	Users register directly on the site with a portal account	Lightweight public portals, small communities, open registration	– Simple to set up – Quick user onboarding	Less secure than enterprise IDPs; avoid for high-security sites
Microsoft Account (Personal Accounts)	Using @outlook. com, @live.com, @hotmail.com	Consumer-facing portals, hobby sites, alumni groups	– No password storage – Broad adoption	Not suitable for enterprise partner access scenarios
Anonymous Access	No sign-in required	Marketing sites, public information pages	– Fastest access – No login friction	Cannot perform authenticated actions (submit secure forms, view personal data)
Custom Identity Providers	Any identity system compliant with OAuth 2.0, OpenID Connect, or SAML	Organizations with legacy or industry-specific ID systems	– Maximum flexibility – Fits unique identity architectures	Requires advanced configuration and security validation

How They Work Together

- **Authentication**: Identifies the user

- **Web Roles**: Assign them a security identity within the site

- **Table Permissions**: Enforce record-level Dataverse access

This three-layer model ensures

- Strong security

- Least-privilege access

- Granular control for external audiences

Governance and Compliance Basics

Power Pages is part of the Microsoft Power Platform, which means it inherits the governance, security, monitoring, and compliance capabilities built into the broader ecosystem. For organizations deploying external-facing sites, having a clear governance structure is essential to maintain security, protect customer data, and ensure consistency across environments. Two fundamental components of this governance model are the **role of administrators** and an understanding of **Power Pages Application Lifecycle Management (ALM)**.

Role of Administrators

Administrators play a central role in maintaining the stability, security, and compliance of Power Pages environments. They are responsible for overseeing how environments are created, who has access to them, and how data and security policies are enforced.

Key Responsibilities of Administrators

Environment Management

- Create, configure, and maintain environments for development, testing, and production.

- Enable or restrict Power Pages capabilities within each environment.

- Ensure Dataverse is provisioned correctly and is compliant with organizational policies.

Security and Access Control

- Manage environment-level permissionsCreate, configure, and maintain environments for development, testing, and production.

- for makers, developers, and users.

- Review and enforce security models such as table permissions, web roles, and authentication providers.

- Configure data loss prevention (DLP) policies that govern connectors and integrations.

Compliance and Monitoring

- Use the Power Platform Admin Center to monitor site usage, performance, and capacity.

- Ensure that the organization complies with shared responsibility models for security.

- Work with governance frameworks like Microsoft Purview, audit logs, retention policies, and data residency requirements.

Change and Release Oversight

- Approve movement of solutions between development, test, and production environments.

- Coordinate deployments with makers and developers to avoid service disruptions.

Administrators act as stewards of both the technical and compliance aspects of Power Pages, balancing agility for makers with the guardrails necessary for secure application development.

Power Pages ALM Overview

Application Lifecycle Management (ALM) provides a structured approach for building, testing, deploying, and maintaining Power Pages solutions. Because Power Pages sites are deeply tied to Dataverse, they follow the same ALM patterns as model-driven apps, custom tables, and flows.

Understanding Power Pages ALM early helps teams avoid ad-hoc development and ensures that portal configurations move reliably between environments.

What ALM Means for Power Pages

ALM ensures that

- Development happens in a dedicated **Dev** environment

- Testing, validation, and stakeholder review occur in a **Test/UAT** environment

- Only approved changes reach **Production**

Key Components of Power Pages ALM

Solutions

Power Pages sites must be packaged in **Dataverse solutions** to support versioning and migration.

Solutions contain

- Web pages

- Web files

- Table permissions

- Web roles

- Forms and views

- Liquid templates

- Site settings

By packaging these components together, teams ensure consistent deployment across environments.

Source Control Integration

Using the Power Platform CLI and source control (like GitHub or Azure DevOps), administrators and developers can store site configuration, templates, and code artifacts in repositories.

This supports

- Version history

- Collaboration

- Rollback capabilities

Deployment Pipelines

Power Platform Pipelines (built-in DevOps capabilities) enable

- Automated deployment of solutions between environments

- Approval workflows

- Controlled promotion from Dev → Test → Production

Pipelines reduce manual errors and enforce governance policies.

Environment Separation

Proper ALM requires physically separated environments:

- **Development**: Makers build pages, forms, templates, and logic.

- **Test/UAT**: Stakeholders validate changes in a controlled environment.

- **Production**: Final approved site goes live to external users.

This separation ensures that experiments or in-progress changes do not disrupt live sites.

Compliance Through ALM

Because ALM provides traceability, auditability, and control, it supports organizational compliance requirements such as

- Change management documentation

- Role-based access during deployments

- Controlled release processes

- Audit logs of who performed what actions

Chapter Summary

- Power Pages is a secure, low-code platform for building external-facing, data-driven websites connected to Microsoft Dataverse.

- It integrates tightly with the broader Power Platform, enabling automation (Power Automate), data visualization (Power BI), and advanced development (CLI, VS Code).

- The Design Studio and built-in templates enable makers to create responsive, professional websites quickly without deep coding skills.

- Pro-developer capabilities, including Liquid, Web APIs, code components, and GitHub integration, support advanced customization.

- Power Pages evolved from Power Apps Portals, introducing stronger security defaults, new admin experiences, and improved design capabilities.

- A site's core architecture includes sites, Dataverse tables, web roles, and web files, all working together to deliver secure, interactive experiences.

- Authentication types such as Azure AD/Entra ID, external IDPs, local accounts, and anonymous access determine how users sign in.

- Web roles + table permissions enforce granular, least-privilege access to pages and data.

- Proper governance requires administrators to manage environments, enforce DLP policies, monitor usage, and ensure compliance.

- Application Lifecycle Management (ALM) helps teams move solutions safely across Dev, Test, and Production environments using solutions and pipelines.

- A correct environment setup, licensing, trial/developer environments, and Dataverse provisioning, is essential before building your first site.

- Power Pages' strengths, low-code building, AI-assisted creation, and responsive design, allow teams to deliver modern websites rapidly and securely.

Practice Exercise

The following exercise helps you put into practice the foundational concepts learned in this chapter. By completing these steps, you will prepare your environment, explore the interface, and validate your understanding of security and governance basics.

Exercise 1: Set Up Your Environment

1. Create a **Trial Environment** or a **Developer Environment** using the Power Apps Developer Plan.

2. Verify that **Dataverse** is provisioned.

3. Open **Power Pages Home** and ensure your new environment appears in the environment selector.

   Goal: Confirm you have a working environment that supports Dataverse and Power Pages.

Exercise 2: Explore the Design Studio

1. Create a new site using a **starter template** (such as "Starter Portal" or "Blank Site").

2. Open the **Design Studio** and complete the following:

   - Add a new page under the main navigation.

   - Modify the homepage title and description.

   - Explore the **Styling** workspace and apply a different theme or brand color.

Goal: Familiarize yourself with the Pages and Styling workspaces.

Exercise 3: Review Dataverse Components

1. Open the **Data workspace** within the Design Studio.

2. Locate the **Contact**, **Account**, and **Web Roles** tables.

3. Create a simple **custom table** (e.g., "Feedback" or "Registration").

4. Add a few sample columns to your table (text, choice, date, etc.).

Goal: Understand how Dataverse tables support your site's data model.

Exercise 4: Investigate Authentication Options

1. Navigate to the **Setup** workspace and explore authentication settings.

2. Identify the default authentication method configured for your site.

3. Review the available authentication providers (local sign-in, Microsoft Entra ID, external IDPs).

Goal: Learn how Power Pages handles sign-in and identity management.

CHAPTER 2

Designing and Building with Copilot and Low-Code

Chapter Objectives

Modern business websites are no longer static collections of pages. They are interactive, data-driven experiences that must be visually consistent, responsive across devices, and quick to build and update. This chapter introduces you to the end-to-end process of creating and styling websites using Power Pages, focusing on the new Design Studio, template-driven development, and AI-powered Copilot capabilities.

In this chapter, you will move beyond basic site creation and learn how to design professional-grade pages visually, organize navigation effectively, apply consistent branding, and accelerate development using AI assistance. The emphasis is on low-code, hands-on building, allowing both technical and non-technical readers to confidently design real-world websites without writing traditional frontend code.

You will start by understanding the structure and purpose of the Design Studio and its workspaces. From there, you will progressively work through page creation, layout design using sections and components, navigation management, styling and theming, and finally AI-assisted generation of forms and content. Each concept builds on the previous one, ensuring a smooth learning curve. Figure 2-1 shows the workspace of Power Pages.

© Dr. Gomathi S, Jerald Felix 2026
Dr. Gomathi S and J. Felix, *Getting Started with Microsoft Power Pages*,
https://doi.org/10.1007/979-8-8688-2667-2_2

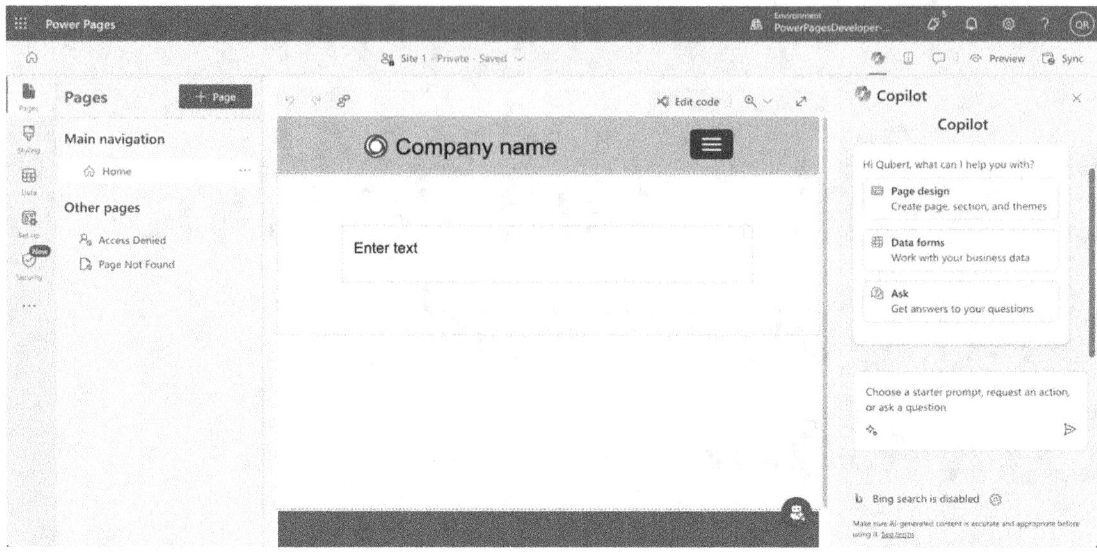

Figure 2-1. *Power Pages Design Overview*

This chapter is intentionally **practical in nature**. Concepts are explained using visuals, tables, and examples that mirror real business scenarios such as landing pages, information portals, and data collection pages. By the end of the chapter, you will not only understand how Power Pages works but also be able to **apply best practices** that result in clean layouts, intuitive navigation, and consistent branding.

What You Will Learn in This Chapter

By completing this chapter, you will be able to

- Understand the role of the **Design Studio** in building Power Pages sites

- Create and manage pages using the **Pages workspace**

- Organize site navigation and page hierarchy for better user experience

- Design page layouts visually using **sections and components**

- Apply themes, colors, and fonts using the **Styling workspace**

- Build sites faster using **prebuilt templates**

- Use **AI-powered Copilot** to generate pages, forms, and text content

- Combine manual design, templates, and AI responsibly for real-world projects

Evolution of the Power Pages Design Experience

The design experience in Power Pages has evolved significantly to address a simple but important goal. Enable anyone to build secure, professional, data-driven websites quickly, without deep web development expertise. Understanding this evolution helps readers appreciate why the **new Design Studio** exists and how it improves productivity, usability, and governance compared to earlier approaches.

From Traditional Portals to Visual Website Building

Power Pages originated from earlier portal technologies that were powerful but complex. Initial experiences relied heavily on configuration screens, separate management apps, and manual coordination between layout, content, and styling. While flexible, this approach often required advanced knowledge of portal metadata, navigation entities, and custom scripts, which slowed down adoption for non-developers.

Page creation was fragmented. Makers frequently switched between multiple tools to

- Create pages

- Configure navigation

- Apply branding

- Preview results

This made simple changes feel heavy and increased the risk of inconsistencies across the site.

The Shift Toward a Unified Design Studio

To reduce complexity, Microsoft introduced a **modern, unified Design Studio** that brings all core site-building tasks into a single visual experience. This marked a major shift in philosophy. Website creation became **visual-first, low-code, and context-aware**.

Instead of configuring pages indirectly, makers now design directly on a live canvas. What you see while editing closely matches what users see at runtime. This WYSIWYG approach significantly shortens feedback loops and improves confidence while building. Figure 2-2 illustrates the Power Pages Design Studio interface, highlighting the page editor in preview mode.

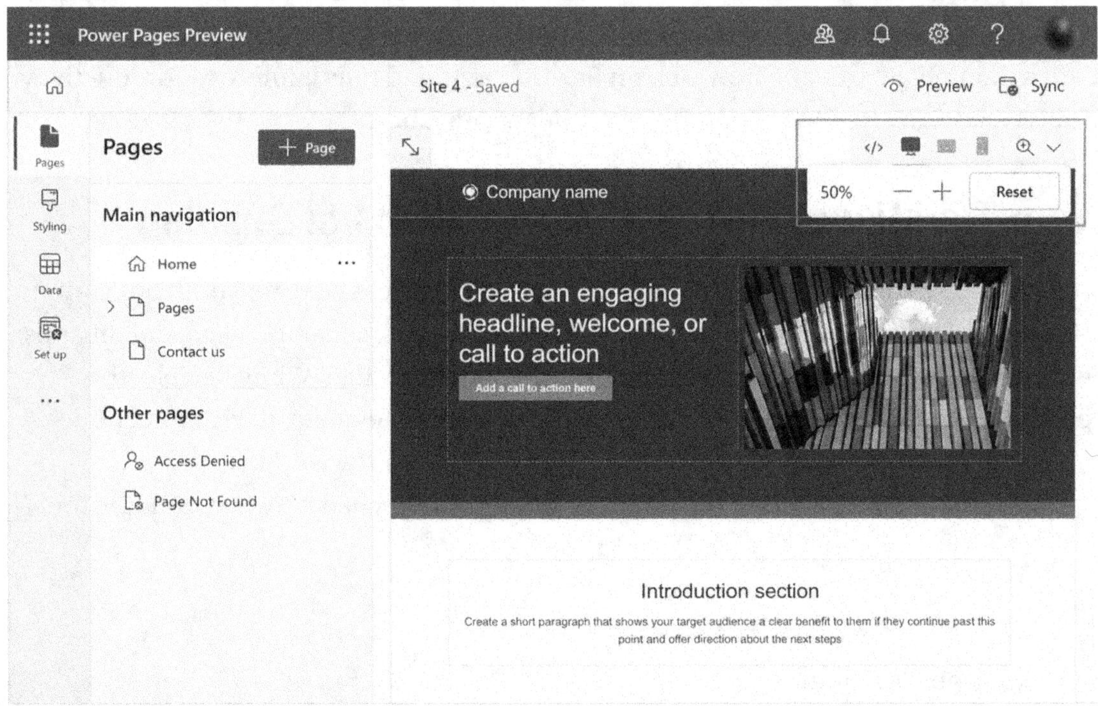

Figure 2-2. *Power Pages Design Studio—Page Editor with Preview and Zoom Controls*

Key Improvements in the Modern Design Experience

The evolution of Power Pages design can be summarized through several key improvements.

Visual-First Page Creation

Pages are now created and edited visually. Layouts are built using sections and components rather than manual markup or scattered settings. This makes the experience intuitive for business users while still structured enough for enterprise needs.

Workspace-Based Organization

Design tasks are clearly separated into focused workspaces:

- Pages for layout, navigation, and content

- Styling for branding and themes

- Data for forms and lists

- Setup for authentication and configuration

This separation reduces confusion and enforces best practices without limiting flexibility.

Table 2-1 compares the earlier portal experience with the modern Power Pages Design Studio, highlighting improvements in page creation, navigation, layout design, styling, learning curve, and overall productivity through a more visual and user-friendly development approach.

Table 2-1. *Comparison Between Earlier Portal Experience and Modern Power Pages Design Studio*

Area	Earlier Portal Experience	Modern Power Pages Design Studio
Page creation	Metadata-driven, indirect	Visual, WYSIWYG editing
Navigation management	Separate configuration screens	Drag-and-drop page hierarchy
Layout design	Limited visual feedback	Sections and components on canvas
Styling	Manual CSS or theme edits	Centralized Styling workspace
Learning curve	Steep for non-developers	Friendly for beginners
Productivity	Slower iteration cycles	Faster build and preview

This comparison highlights why the modern experience is more approachable while still enterprise-ready.

Introduction of Templates and Starter Experiences

Another major milestone in the evolution was the introduction of **template-driven site creation**. Instead of starting from a blank site, makers can now choose from prebuilt templates designed for common business scenarios such as registrations, applications, and information portals. Figure 2-3 illustrates the Power Pages template gallery, showcasing a collection of prebuilt starter layouts designed to accelerate website creation.

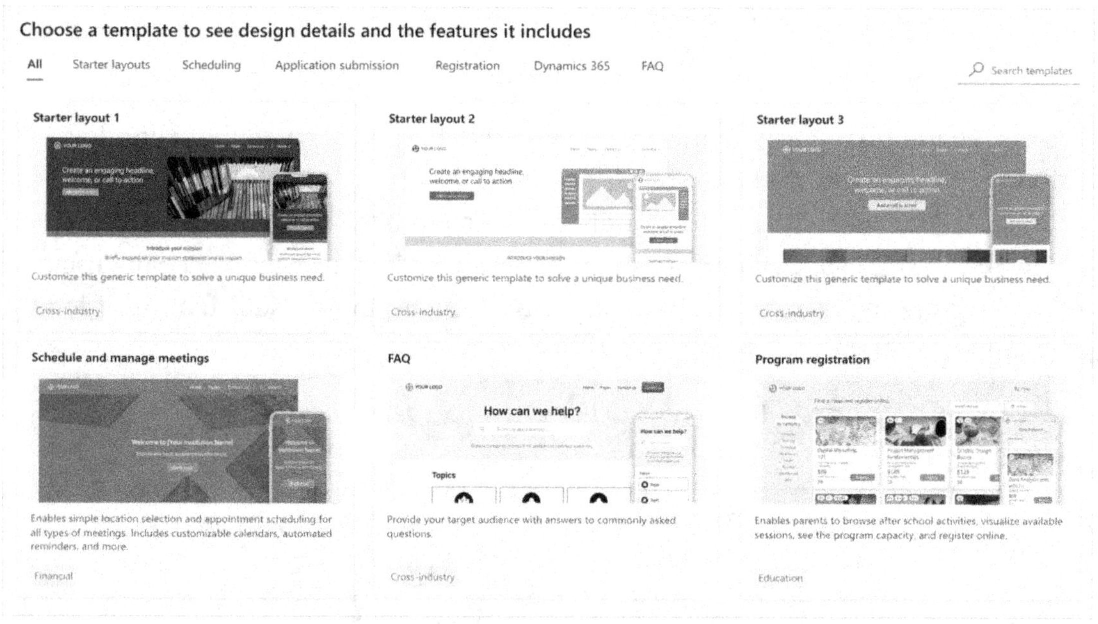

Figure 2-3. *Power Pages Template Gallery and Starter Layouts*

Templates provide

- Predefined page structures

- Sample navigation

- Consistent layout patterns

This reduces setup time and helps beginners learn best practices by example.

The Role of AI and Copilot in Design Evolution

The most recent and transformative change in the Power Pages design experience is the integration of **AI-powered Copilot**. Copilot introduces natural language interaction into the design process. Figure 2-4 shows the Power Automate home page highlighting the Copilot-assisted automation experience.

Instead of manually creating everything, makers can now

- Describe the website they want to build

- Generate page structures automatically

- Create forms and text content using prompts

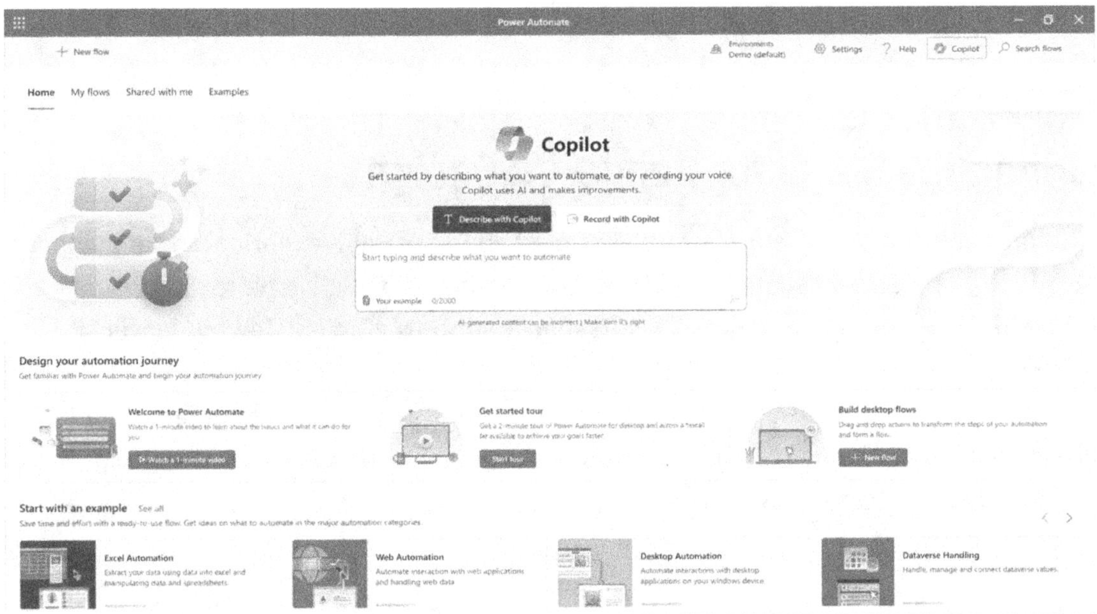

Figure 2-4. *Power Automate Home Page with Copilot Experience*

This does not replace manual design. Instead, it acts as an accelerator, helping makers overcome blank-page syndrome and focus on refinement rather than setup.

Why This Evolution Matters to Readers

The evolution of the Power Pages design experience is not just cosmetic. It directly impacts how quickly and safely websites can be built.

Key benefits for readers include

- Faster learning curve for beginners

- Reduced dependency on professional web developers

- More consistent and maintainable designs

- Better alignment with enterprise governance and branding

- Improved collaboration between business users and IT teams

Tip   Use the modern Design Studio as your primary tool. Older management experiences are still useful for advanced scenarios, but day-to-day page design is faster and safer in the visual editor.

Setting the Stage for Hands-On Design

With the evolution complete, Power Pages now offers a design experience that balances **simplicity, power, and scalability.** In the next section, you will explore the Design Studio itself and understand how its workspaces support efficient, low-code website creation.

This foundation ensures that when you start building pages, managing navigation, and styling layouts, you are working within a modern, purpose-built environment designed for real-world business needs.

Introduction to the Power Pages Design Studio

The Power Pages Design Studio is the **central workspace where all website creation and customization happen.** It is designed to give makers a unified, visual, and low-code experience for building professional websites without switching between multiple tools. Whether you are creating pages, adjusting layouts, applying branding, or using AI assistance, the Design Studio acts as your single control center.

At its core, the Design Studio follows a **what-you-see-is-what-you-get** approach. The canvas you edit closely represents the final user experience, allowing you to design with confidence and reduce trial-and-error during development.

The Design Studio interface is intentionally divided into clearly defined areas:

- **Left navigation pane** for pages and workspaces

- **Central canvas** for live page editing

- **Right-side Copilot panel** for AI-assisted guidance and generation

- **Top command bar** for previewing, syncing, and publishing

This layout helps makers stay focused and work efficiently without losing context. Figure 2-5 presents the core philosophy behind the Design Studio, emphasizing three foundational principles that guide the page-building experience.

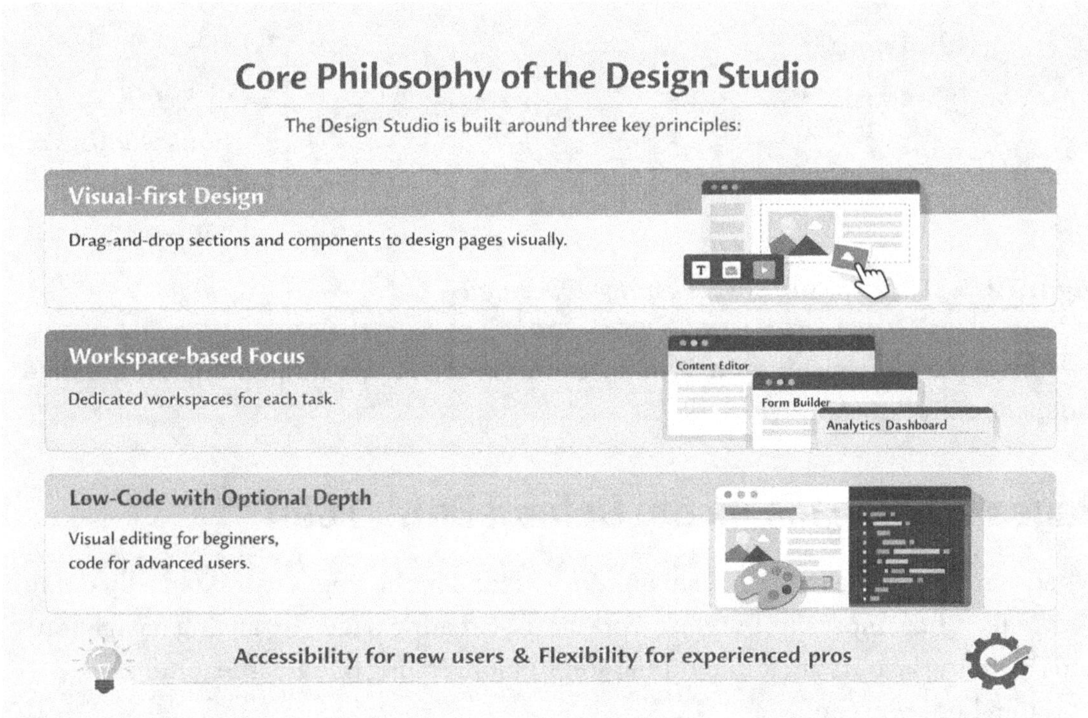

Figure 2-5. *Core Philosophy of the Design Studio*

Understanding Design Studio Workspaces

The Design Studio is organized into four primary workspaces, each responsible for a specific aspect of site building. Figure 2-6 provides an overview of the Design Studio workspace, illustrating how core capabilities are organized around a central design environment.

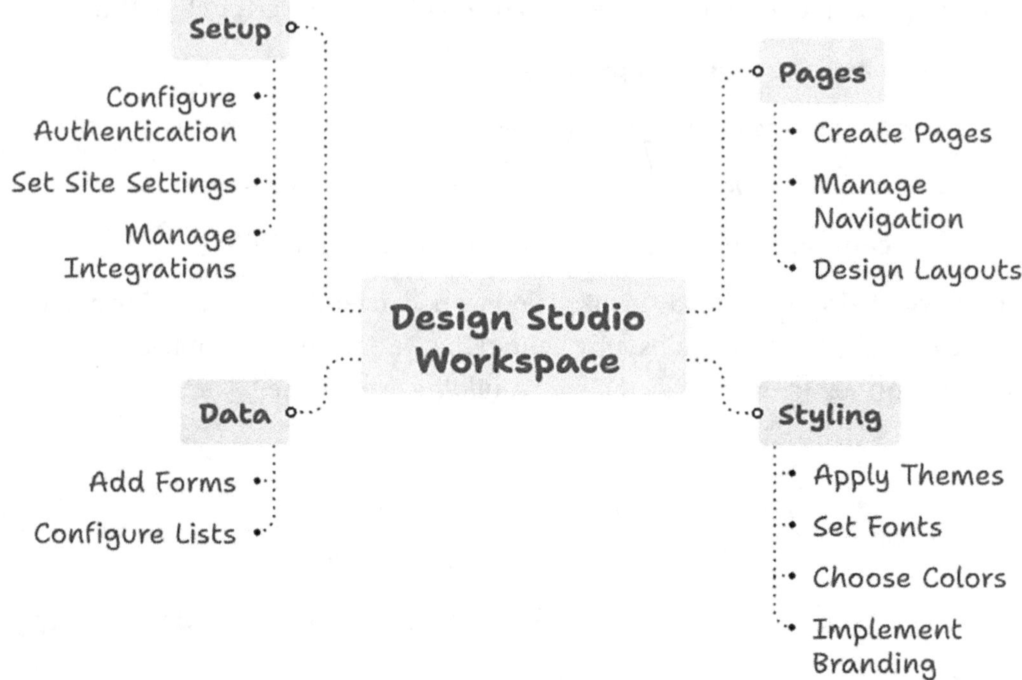

Figure 2-6. *Design Studio Workspace Overview*

This separation ensures that layout, branding, data, and configuration are handled independently but cohesively.

Pages Workspace as the Default Entry Point

When you open a site in the Design Studio, you land in the **Pages workspace by default**. This reflects how most site-building work starts. Creating pages, arranging navigation, and designing layouts are foundational steps before styling or data integration.

From here, you can

- Add and organize pages

- Define navigation structure

- Design layouts using sections and components

- Edit page content directly on the canvas

Later sections in this chapter will explore each of these actions in detail.

The Live Editing Canvas

The central canvas is where the Design Studio truly shines. It allows **in-context editing**, meaning changes are made directly where content appears.

You can

- Click on text and type immediately

- Drag components to reposition them

- Resize images visually

- Select sections to adjust layout properties

This real-time feedback eliminates guesswork and makes design intuitive, especially for users without frontend development experience.

Built-In Preview Options

The Design Studio includes built-in preview tools that help validate your design before publishing.

You can preview

- Desktop view in a new browser tab

- Mobile view using a QR code

- Mobile preview via email link

These options ensure your site looks and behaves correctly across devices.

Copilot Integration Within the Design Studio

A defining feature of the modern Design Studio is the presence of **AI-powered Copilot**, available directly within the interface.

Copilot can assist with

- Generating page layouts

- Creating forms

- Writing text content

- Answering "how-to" questions while designing

Copilot works alongside you, not instead of you. Makers remain in full control and can accept, modify, or discard AI-generated suggestions.

Tip   Use the Design Studio as your primary workspace for daily site-building tasks. Switch to advanced tools only when necessary to avoid unnecessary complexity.

Understanding the Pages Workspace

The **Pages workspace** is where most of your hands-on design work happens in Power Pages. It is the primary environment for creating pages, organizing navigation, and shaping the overall structure of your website. If the Design Studio is the control center, the Pages workspace is the construction site where the site takes form.

This workspace is intentionally designed to be **visual, intuitive, and incremental**, allowing makers to build pages step by step while always seeing the final result.

Pages Workspace at a Glance

The Pages workspace is composed of three key areas:

1. **Pages and navigation pane** on the left

2. **Live editing canvas** in the center

3. **Contextual properties and toolbars** on selection

Each area works together to provide a smooth, low-code page-building experience.

Role of the Pages Workspace

The Pages workspace is responsible for **page-level design and structure**, not global styling or deep data configuration. It focuses on how users move through your site and what they see on each page.

In this workspace, you can

- Create new pages and define their URLs

- Control which pages appear in navigation

- Arrange page hierarchy using parent and child pages

- Design page layouts using sections and components

- Edit content directly on the canvas

This makes it the natural starting point for building any Power Pages site.

Pages and Navigation Pane

On the left side of the workspace, you see the **Pages pane**, which displays the site structure in a tree-like format.

This pane shows

- Top-level pages in the main navigation

- Nested pages that appear as dropdown menus

- Pages hidden from navigation but still accessible

You can quickly understand how your site is organized without opening individual pages.

Page Types and Visibility

When adding a page, you decide how it should appear and how users should access it.

Table 2-2. *Page Locations and Their Usage in Power Pages*

Page Location	Description	Typical Use
Main navigation	Visible in the site header	Home, About, Services
Subpage	Nested under a parent page	FAQs, Details pages
Other pages	Hidden from main menu	Thank-you pages, redirects

This flexibility allows you to design clean navigation while still supporting pages behind the scenes.

Managing Page Hierarchy Visually

The Pages workspace makes navigation management visual rather than configuration-heavy. Using the ellipsis (⋯) menu next to each page, you can

- Move pages up or down to change menu order

- Convert a page into a subpage

- Promote a subpage to top level

- Duplicate a page layout

- Delete pages safely

Table 2-3. Page Actions and Their Impact on Navigation in Power Pages

Action	Result
Make subpage	Creates dropdown navigation
Promote subpage	Moves page to main level
Duplicate page	Reuses layout and components
Move up / down	Adjusts menu order

Tip   Plan your navigation structure before adding content. A clear hierarchy reduces rework and improves user experience.

The Live Page Canvas

The center of the Pages workspace is the **live canvas**, where you design pages visually. This canvas always reflects the current page and updates in real time as you make changes.

On the canvas, you can

- Click directly on text to edit

- Add sections and components visually

- Rearrange elements using drag and drop

- Select elements to access their settings

This eliminates the disconnect between design and preview that exists in traditional web development tools.

In-Context Editing Experience

All page edits happen **in context**, meaning

- Text is edited where it appears

- Buttons are configured inline

- Images are resized visually

- Section layouts are adjusted live

This approach reduces mistakes and speeds up iteration.

Pages Workspace vs. Other Workspaces

Understanding the boundaries of the Pages workspace prevents confusion later.

Table 2-4. *Comparison of Pages Workspace and Other Workspaces in Power Pages*

Task	Pages Workspace	Other Workspace
Page layout	Yes	—
Navigation	Yes	—
Page content	Yes	—
Global colors and fonts	No	Styling
Data connections	Limited	Data
Authentication	No	Setup

Tip   Use the Pages workspace for structure and layout decisions. Leave branding and data configuration to their dedicated workspaces.

Why the Pages Workspace Matters

A well-organized Pages workspace leads to

- Cleaner navigation

- Better page structure

- Easier maintenance

- Faster collaboration

By mastering this workspace early, you lay a strong foundation for everything else you build in Power Pages.

Creating Pages in Power Pages

Creating pages is the first hands-on step in building a Power Pages website. Pages represent the **individual screens users navigate to**, such as Home, About, Services, or Contact pages. In Power Pages, page creation is intentionally simple and visual, allowing makers to focus on structure and content rather than technical configuration.

This section walks through **how pages are created, configured, and positioned within the site**, using the Pages workspace.

Starting Page Creation

All page creation begins from the **Pages workspace**. From the left navigation pane, you can add a new page with just a few clicks. Figure 2-7 shows the Pages workspace in the Power Pages Design Studio, highlighting the option to create a new page using the + **Page** button.

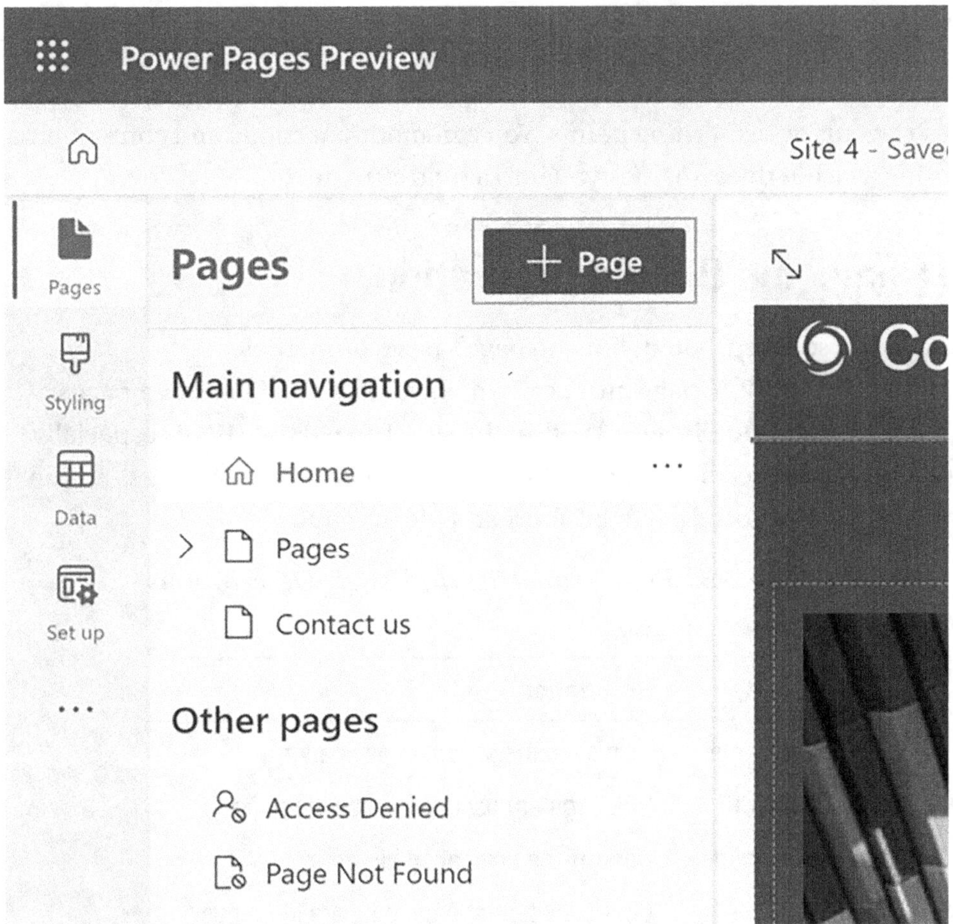

Figure 2-7. *Creating a New Page in Power Pages Design Studio*

When you choose to add a page, Power Pages prompts you to select how the page should be created. You can either start from a **predefined layout** or use a **blank page** for full control.

Choosing a Page Layout

Power Pages provides ready-made page layouts to speed up development and encourage best practices.

Common layout options include

- **Landing page** for home or overview content

- **Subpage** for secondary information

- **Contact us** or similar informational layouts

- **Blank page** for custom designs

These layouts act as starting points. You can modify sections and components later, so choosing a layout does not lock you into a rigid structure.

Page Name and URL Configuration

Once a layout is selected, you define the page's basic properties.

As shown in Table 2-5, page properties in Power Pages define how a page is identified, accessed, and displayed within the site. The **partial URL** is especially important because it becomes part of the site's web address. Power Pages automatically formats it, but you can adjust it to be short and meaningful.

Table 2-5. *Page Properties and Their Descriptions in Power Pages*

Property	Description
Page name	Display name shown in navigation
Partial URL	URL segment used to access the page
Parent page	Determines navigation hierarchy
Visibility	Controls whether page appears in menus

Tip   Use simple, readable URLs. For example, use /services instead of /our-company-services-page.

Controlling Page Visibility

Power Pages allows you to control where and how pages appear in the site navigation. You can choose to place pages in

- **Main navigation**, making them visible in the site header

- **Other pages**, keeping them hidden from the main menu

Hidden pages are still accessible via direct links, buttons, or redirects, which is useful for thank-you pages, confirmation screens, or internal flows.

Figure 2-8 illustrates the overall website navigation and page placement structure within a Power Pages site. The diagram shows how website navigation is organized into three primary categories. The Main Navigation includes core user-facing pages such as Home, About, and Services, which are directly accessible from the site menu. Subpages are used to group related content, such as FAQs and detail pages, under a parent page to maintain a logical hierarchy. Other Pages consist of system and utility pages like Thank-You and error pages, which are not typically visible in the main navigation. This structured navigation model helps improve user experience by ensuring clear content organization and intuitive site navigation. This separation helps maintain clean navigation while supporting functional page flows.

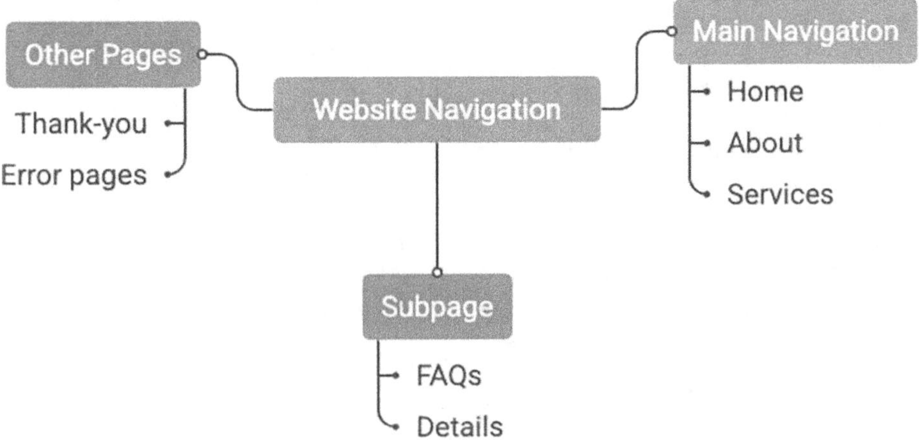

Figure 2-8. *Website Navigation and Page Placement Structure*

Setting Parent and Child Pages

During creation, or later through page settings, you can define a **parent page**. This creates a parent–child relationship that appears as nested navigation or dropdown menus.

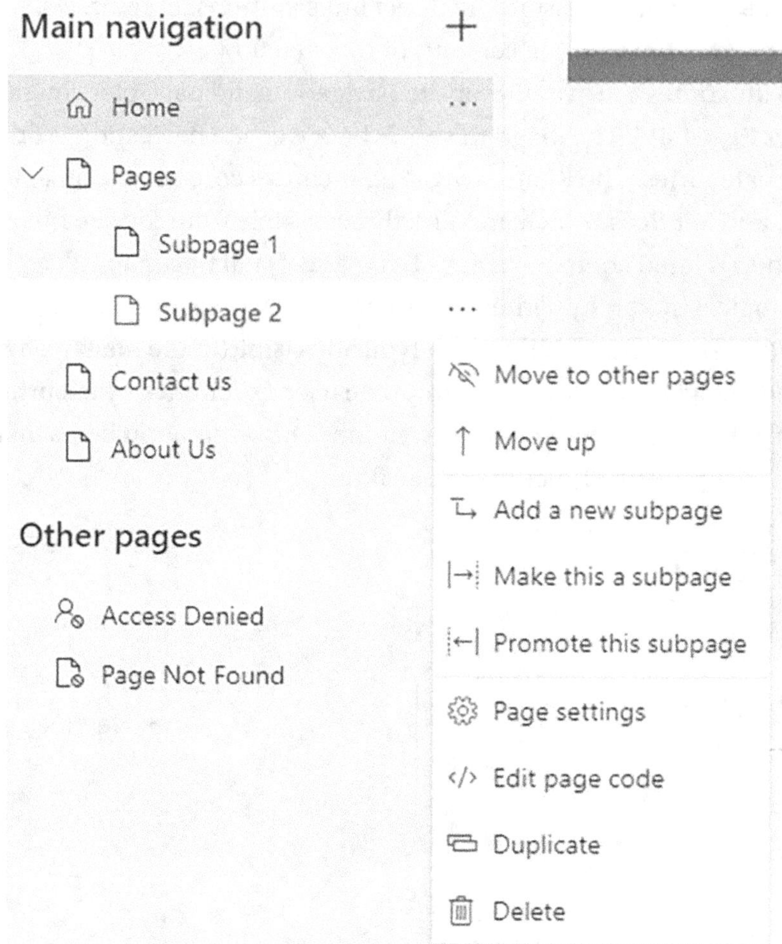

Figure 2-9. *Managing Pages and Subpages in Power Pages Navigation*

This structure is essential for organizing larger sites with multiple content sections. Figure 2-9 shows the page management options available within the Main navigation section of the Power Pages Design Studio. The navigation tree displays parent pages and their associated subpages, providing a clear hierarchical view of the site structure. By selecting the context menu for a page, makers can move pages up or down, add new subpages, convert a page into a subpage, or promote a subpage to a top-level page. Additional options such as page settings, editing page code, duplicating, and deleting pages enable efficient maintenance and restructuring of the website. This flexible navigation management helps ensure that site content remains well organized and easy for users to navigate.

Tip Limit navigation depth to two levels whenever possible. Deep nesting can confuse users and reduce usability.

Creating Pages Incrementally

Power Pages encourages **incremental page creation**. You do not need to fully design a page at creation time.

A common workflow is

1. Create all required pages first

2. Organize navigation and hierarchy

3. Design layouts and content page by page

This approach prevents rework and ensures consistent structure across the site.

Duplicating Pages for Faster Builds

Once a page is created and styled, you can duplicate it to reuse the layout and components.

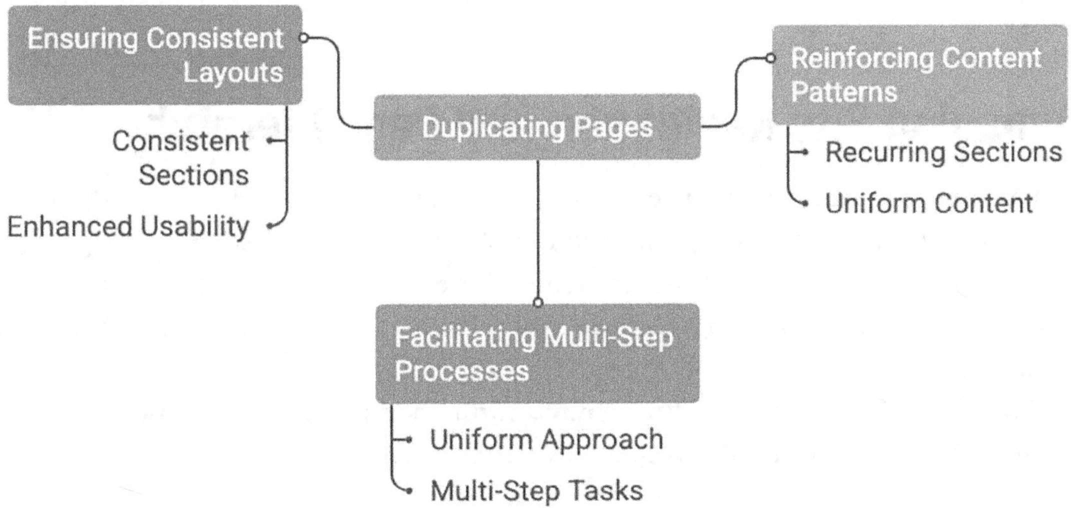

Figure 2-10. Benefits of Duplicating Pages in Power Pages

Figure 2-10 explains the advantages of duplicating pages within Power Pages. Duplicating pages helps ensure consistent layouts by reusing predefined sections and design elements, which improves overall usability and visual coherence across the site. It also reinforces content patterns by allowing recurring sections and uniform content structures to be applied across multiple pages. In addition, page duplication facilitates multistep processes by providing a uniform approach for creating sequential or related pages, such as forms or guided workflows. This capability reduces design effort, saves time, and helps maintain a consistent user experience throughout the website.

Deleting and Cleaning Up Pages

Pages that are no longer required can be safely removed from the Pages workspace. Deleting a page removes it from navigation and makes it inaccessible to users.

Before deleting, always verify

- The page is not referenced by buttons or links

- The page is not part of an active user flow

Tip   If you are unsure, duplicate the page before deleting. This provides a backup without impacting the live site.

Managing Site Navigation and Page Hierarchy

Site navigation determines **how users move through your website**. Even well-designed pages can feel confusing if navigation is cluttered or poorly structured. Power Pages makes navigation management visual and intuitive through the Pages workspace, allowing makers to organize pages, create logical hierarchies, and adjust menus without writing code.

This section focuses on **structuring navigation, managing parent–child relationships, and maintaining a clean menu experience**.

Understanding Navigation in Power Pages

Navigation in Power Pages is driven directly by the **page hierarchy** you define in the Pages workspace. There is no separate navigation editor. The way pages are arranged in the Pages pane determines how menus appear on the site.

At a high level:

- **Top-level pages** appear in the main navigation bar.

- **Child pages** appear as dropdown items.

- **Hidden pages** remain accessible but do not appear in menus.

This tight connection between pages and navigation reduces configuration effort and improves consistency.

The Pages Tree View

The Pages pane displays your site structure as a **nested tree view**. This visual representation allows you to understand the entire navigation layout at a glance.

You can immediately identify

- Which pages are visible in the main menu

- Which pages are grouped under a parent

- How deep the navigation hierarchy goes

This is especially useful for medium to large sites where navigation clarity is critical.

Reordering Pages in Navigation

The order of pages in the Pages pane directly controls the order of menu items on the site. Using the ellipsis (···) menu next to each page, you can reorder pages easily.

Common actions include

- **Move up** to shift a page left in the menu

- **Move down** to shift a page right in the menu

These changes are reflected immediately in the navigation preview.

Using "Other Pages" for Cleaner Navigation

Not every page should appear in the main menu. Power Pages allows you to place pages under **Other pages**, keeping them hidden from navigation.

Hidden pages are commonly used for

- Thank-you or confirmation pages

- Redirect targets

- Error or access-denied pages

- Pages accessed only through buttons or links

This keeps the main navigation focused and user-friendly.

Designing Navigation for User Experience

When organizing navigation, always think from the user's perspective.

Best practices include

- Group related pages under a single parent

- Use clear, short page names

- Avoid duplicate or overlapping menu items

- Prioritize frequently used pages

Tip   If users need to think about where to click next, navigation needs improvement.

Navigation Changes and Live Preview

All navigation changes can be previewed instantly using the built-in preview options. This allows you to verify

- Menu order

- Dropdown behavior

- Mobile responsiveness

Always preview navigation on both desktop and mobile views to ensure usability across devices.

Pages Workspace and Navigation Scope

It is important to remember what the Pages workspace controls and what it does not.

Navigation controls *where users can go*, not *what they are allowed to access*. Security is enforced separately through roles and permissions. As outlined in Table 2-6, the Pages workspace in Power Pages is responsible for controlling the menu structure, page order, dropdown hierarchy, and page visibility. However, aspects such as page security, role-based access, styling and colors, and authentication rules are managed in other areas of the Power Pages environment. This clear division ensures that navigation design and security configuration remain organized and easy to maintain.

Table 2-6. *Navigation Controls Managed in Pages Workspace vs. Other Areas*

Controlled Here	Controlled Elsewhere
Menu structure	Page security
Page order	Role-based access
Dropdown hierarchy	Styling and colors
Page visibility	Authentication rules

Designing Pages with Sections, Components, and Content

Designing pages in Power Pages is a **hands-on, visual process** built around low-code building blocks. Instead of writing HTML or CSS, you compose pages by adding **sections**, placing **components**, and editing **content directly on the canvas**. This approach lets you design professional, responsive pages quickly while staying focused on structure and clarity.

At a conceptual level, every page follows a simple hierarchy:

Page → Sections → Components → Content

Once you understand this model, page design becomes predictable, repeatable, and easy to maintain.

Page Composition Model—How Everything Fits Together

- **Page:** The full screen users see

- **Sections:** Horizontal layout containers

- **Components:** Functional elements inside sections

- **Content:** Text, media, or data edited in place

Step 1: Creating Layouts Using Sections

Sections form the **structural backbone** of a page. Each section defines how content is arranged horizontally and provides a container for components.

When adding a section, you select a column layout such as

- One column for focused content

- Two columns for side-by-side layouts

- Three columns for features or comparisons

Each section can be configured using the property panel to control alignment, background color, and spacing.

Common Section Layouts and Use Cases

Table 2-7. *Section Layout Options and Their Typical Use Cases in Power Pages*

Section Layout	Typical Use
One column	Headings, hero text, long content
Two columns	Image + text, form + description
Three columns	Features, services, highlights
Full-width	Banners, announcements

Tip   Always add and finalize sections first. Once the layout feels right, adding components becomes much easier.

Step 2: Adding Components to Sections

Components are the **building blocks that bring a page to life.** After selecting a section, you drag and drop components from the component library into the section.

Power Pages provides two broad categories of components.

Table 2-8. *Content Components*

Component	Purpose
Text	Headings, paragraphs, instructions
Image	Banners, illustrations, logos
Button	Navigation and calls to action
Video	Embedded media
Spacer	Controls vertical spacing
Divider	Separates content visually

Table 2-9. *Data Components*

Component	Purpose
List	Displays multiple Dataverse records
Basic Form	Create or edit a single record
Multistep Form	Guided data entry across steps

Data components connect directly to Microsoft Dataverse and render live business data to users.

Tip   Use content components for layout and messaging first. Add data components only when the page flow is clear.

Step 3: Editing Content Directly on the Canvas

One of the most powerful features of the Pages workspace is **in-context editing**. You work directly on the page instead of configuring content in separate dialogs.

You can

- Click text and start typing immediately

- Resize images by dragging their corners

- Change button labels and links inline

- Adjust alignment and spacing visually

This ensures what you design is exactly what users will experience.

Tip   Avoid placeholder text for too long. Real content helps you judge spacing, readability, and layout accuracy.

Step 4: Combining Sections and Components Effectively

Good page design is about **clarity and balance**, not adding more components.

Recommended Page Structure Pattern

Table 2-10. *Recommended Page Structure by Page Area in Power Pages*

Page Area	Suggested Structure
Header	Section + Text + Button
Main content	Multiple sections with mixed layouts
Data entry	Section + Form + supporting text
Supporting info	Section + Text or List

Visual Example: Typical Business Page Layout

Understanding Scope. What Pages Workspace Controls

It is important to clearly separate responsibilities between workspaces.

Table 2-11. *Responsibilities of Pages Workspace vs. Styling Workspace in Power Pages*

Pages Workspace Handles	Styling Workspace Handles
Page layout	Fonts
Sections and components	Colors
Page-specific content	Themes
Navigation placement	Brand consistency

This separation ensures consistent branding across all pages without manual styling.

Tip   Do not manually style individual components unless necessary. Let the Styling workspace control global appearance.

Accessibility and Responsive Design by Default

All sections and components are **responsive by design**. Pages automatically adapt to mobile, tablet, and desktop screens.

However, good design practices still matter:

- Avoid overcrowding sections

- Use spacers instead of extra line breaks

- Preview pages in desktop and mobile views

Working with Sections for Responsive Layouts

Sections are the **foundation of responsive design** in Power Pages. They control how content is arranged horizontally and how it adapts across different screen sizes. By understanding how sections behave and how to configure them correctly, you can create layouts that look clean and usable on desktops, tablets, and mobile devices without writing any custom CSS.

This section focuses on **using sections effectively to build flexible, responsive layouts**.

Why Sections Matter for Responsiveness

In Power Pages, responsiveness is built into the platform. Sections automatically adjust column widths and stacking behavior based on screen size. This means that a layout designed on a desktop will reorganize itself gracefully on smaller devices.

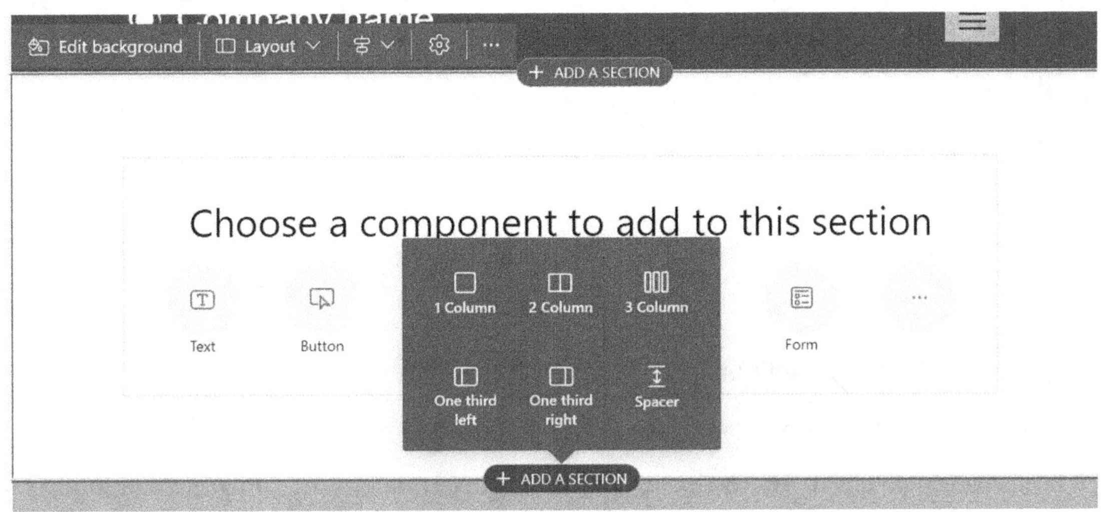

Figure 2-11. *Responsibilities of Pages Workspace vs. Styling Workspace in Power Pages*

For example:

- Two-column sections stack vertically on mobile.

- Full-width sections adapt to screen size.

- Content remains readable without manual adjustments.

Understanding Section Types

Power Pages offers several section layouts that serve different design purposes.

Table 2-12. *Section Types, Descriptions, and Best Use Cases in Power Pages*

Section Type	Description	Best Use
One-column	Single content area	Headings, long text
Two-column	Side-by-side content	Image + text
Three-column	Equal-width columns	Features, services
Full-width	Spans entire screen	Hero banners

Each section type is responsive by default and adapts based on available screen width.

Adding and Configuring Sections

Sections are added directly from the page canvas. Once a section is selected, its properties can be adjusted using the configuration panel.

Common section settings include

- Background color

- Vertical and horizontal alignment

- Padding and spacing

- Section visibility

These settings allow you to visually separate content areas and improve readability.

Tip   Use background colors sparingly. Alternating light and neutral backgrounds helps users visually scan the page.

Full-Width vs. Contained Sections

Choosing between full-width and contained sections has a major impact on visual hierarchy.

Table 2-13. *Section Styles, Behavior, and Typical Usage in Power Pages*

Section Style	Behavior	Typical Use
Full-width	Extends edge to edge	Hero sections, banners
Contained	Limited to content width	Text-heavy areas

A common pattern is to use

- Full-width sections at the top of the page

- Contained sections for detailed content

Spacing and Visual Balance

Proper spacing improves readability and visual flow. Power Pages provides **spacers and padding controls** to manage vertical space without hacks.

Best practices:

- Use spacers instead of extra blank lines

- Maintain consistent spacing between sections

- Avoid overcrowding sections with too many components

Tip   If a section feels cluttered, split it into two simpler sections rather than adding more columns.

Section Visibility and Page Flow

Sections can be shown or hidden based on design needs. This is useful when

- Temporarily hiding content

- Testing alternate layouts

- Preparing future content

Hidden sections remain part of the page and can be re-enabled later.

Previewing Responsive Behavior

Always preview your page after adding or modifying sections. Power Pages provides built-in preview options for different devices.

Previewing helps verify

- Column stacking behavior

- Text readability on mobile

- Button placement and spacing

Table 2-14 provides common section design mistakes.

Table 2-14. *Common Section Design Mistakes and Their Impact in Power Pages*

Mistake	Impact
Too many columns	Poor mobile readability
Overusing full-width sections	Visual fatigue
Inconsistent spacing	Unpolished appearance
Crowded sections	Reduced usability

Tip   Design for mobile first mentally, even if you build on desktop. Simpler sections translate better across devices.

Using Components to Build Page Content

Components are the **functional elements** that turn a page layout into a meaningful user experience. While sections define *where* content sits, components define *what* users see and interact with. Power Pages provides a rich set of ready-to-use components that allow makers to build engaging, interactive pages without writing code.

This section focuses on **choosing the right components, placing them effectively, and using them to deliver clear, purposeful content**.

Understanding Components in Power Pages

Components are added **inside sections** and can be rearranged, edited, or removed at any time. Each component is designed to handle a specific type of content or interaction, such as displaying text, capturing user input, or navigating between pages.

Power Pages groups components broadly into

- **Content components** for layout and messaging

- **Data components** for interacting with Dataverse data

Figure 2-12 illustrates the process of adding data-connected components within the Power Pages Design Studio. The component picker displays standard components such as Spacer, Image, Search, and Flex container, along with data-connected options. The Summary component, highlighted in the figure, enables makers to surface and display data from underlying data sources directly on a page. This capability allows pages to present dynamic, data-driven content without custom coding, making it easier to build rich, interactive experiences that stay synchronized with backend data.

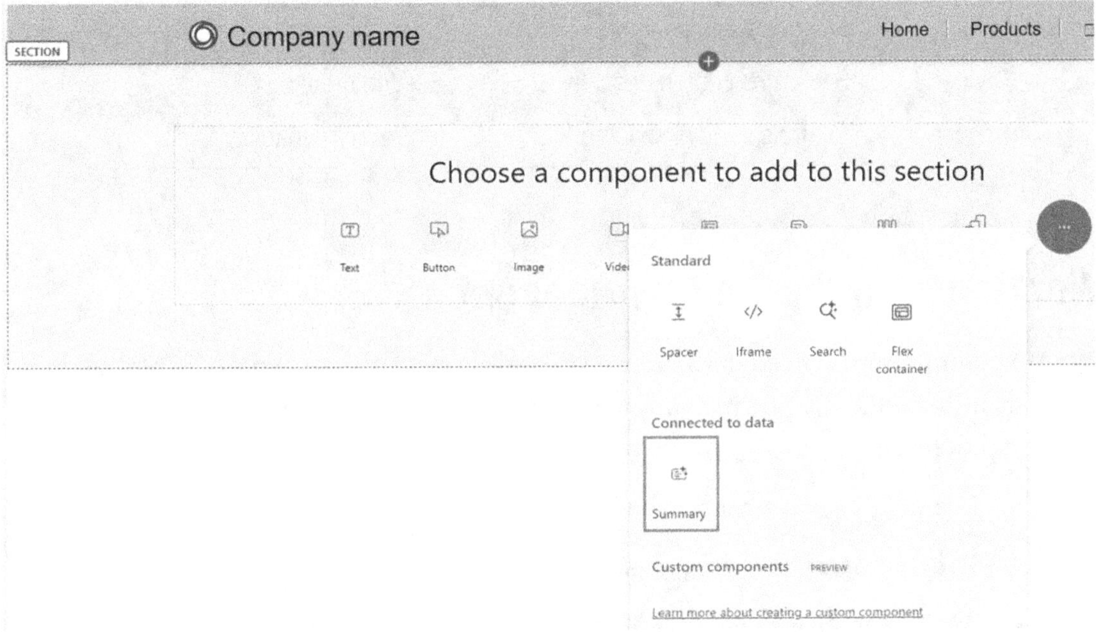

Figure 2-12. Adding Data-Connected Components in Power Pages

Content Components: Building the Visual Experience

Content components are the most commonly used elements on a page. They help communicate information clearly and guide users through the site.

Table 2-15 provides common content components.

Table 2-15. *Common Page Components, Their Purpose, and Typical Usage in Power Pages*

Component	Purpose	Typical Use
Text	Displays headings and paragraphs	Page titles, instructions
Image	Displays images	Banners, illustrations, logos
Button	Triggers navigation or actions	Submit, Learn more
Video	Embeds video content	Tutorials, announcements
Divider	Separates content visually	Section breaks
Spacer	Controls vertical spacing	Improves readability

Working with the Text Component

The **Text** component is used for headings, descriptions, and instructional content. It supports inline editing, allowing you to click directly on the text and start typing.

Best practices:

- Use headings to structure content

- Keep paragraphs short and scannable

- Avoid placing large blocks of text in multi-column sections

Tip   Treat text like a conversation. Short, clear sentences improve readability, especially on mobile devices.

Using Images and Media Effectively

Images and videos enhance visual appeal and reinforce messaging. Power Pages allows you to resize, align, and reposition media directly on the canvas.

Best practices:

- Use optimized images to improve performance

- Avoid using images as text replacements

- Ensure images support the content, not distract from it

Buttons and Calls to Action

Buttons are critical for guiding users through the site. They can link to pages, trigger navigation, or start processes.

Common button uses:

- Navigate to another page

- Open a form or registration page

- Direct users to external resources

Button text should clearly describe the action, such as *Register now* or *View details*.

Data Components. Adding Interactivity with Dataverse

Data components connect your pages directly to **Microsoft Dataverse**, allowing users to view and submit real business data.

Table 2-16. *Key Data Components*

Data Component	What It Does	Best Use
List	Displays multiple records	Dashboards, record overviews
Basic Form	Creates or edits one record	Contact forms, feedback
Multistep Form	Guides users through steps	Applications, onboarding

These components respect table permissions and security settings automatically.

Tip   Always confirm table permissions before publishing pages with data components. A page may load, but data may not display without proper permissions.

Combining Components for Effective Page Design

Effective pages use **a balanced mix of components** rather than relying on a single type.

Table 2-17. Recommended Component Patterns

Page Purpose	Suggested Components
Landing page	Text + Image + Button
Information page	Text + Divider + Image
Data entry page	Text + Form + Button
Overview page	List + Filters + Button

Component Placement and Readability

Good component placement improves user experience.

Guidelines:

- Place important content above the fold

- Align components consistently

- Avoid mixing too many component types in a single section

- Leave sufficient white space

Table 2-18. *Common Component Design Mistakes*

Mistake	Impact
Too many buttons	User confusion
Overusing images	Slower load times
Long text blocks	Poor readability
Crowded sections	Visual overload

Tip   If a section feels busy, remove one component and reassess. Simpler layouts are usually more effective.

Chapter Summary

- This chapter transitions from the foundational concepts in Chapter 1 to hands-on website design and building using Power Pages.

- It introduces the modern Power Pages Design Studio, highlighting its visual, low-code, and workspace-based approach to site creation.

- Readers learn how to create and manage pages, structure navigation, and design layouts using sections and components.

- The chapter explains how responsive, professional pages can be built visually without traditional frontend coding.

- Data-connected components are introduced to display and collect Dataverse data while respecting security and permissions.

- AI-powered Copilot is presented as a productivity accelerator for generating layouts, forms, and content.

- By the end of the chapter, readers can confidently design structured, responsive Power Pages sites and are prepared for deeper data and security integration in later chapters.

CHAPTER 3

Data Integration

Chapter Objectives

In the previous chapter, you learned how to design and style pages visually using the Power Pages Design Studio. Those pages looked great. But a website truly becomes powerful only when it can **store, display, and interact with real data**. That is exactly what this chapter is about.

This chapter focuses on **data integration in Power Pages**. You will learn how to connect your site to data stored in Microsoft Dataverse and expose that data to users through lists and forms. By the end of this chapter, your site will move from content-driven to **data-driven**.

Power Pages makes data integration approachable through a dedicated **Data workspace**. Instead of writing code or building APIs manually, makers work visually with tables, forms, and views that already exist in Dataverse. This chapter shows you how to use those building blocks effectively and safely.

© Dr. Gomathi S, Jerald Felix 2026
Dr. Gomathi S and J. Felix, *Getting Started with Microsoft Power Pages*,
https://doi.org/10.1007/979-8-8688-2667-2_3

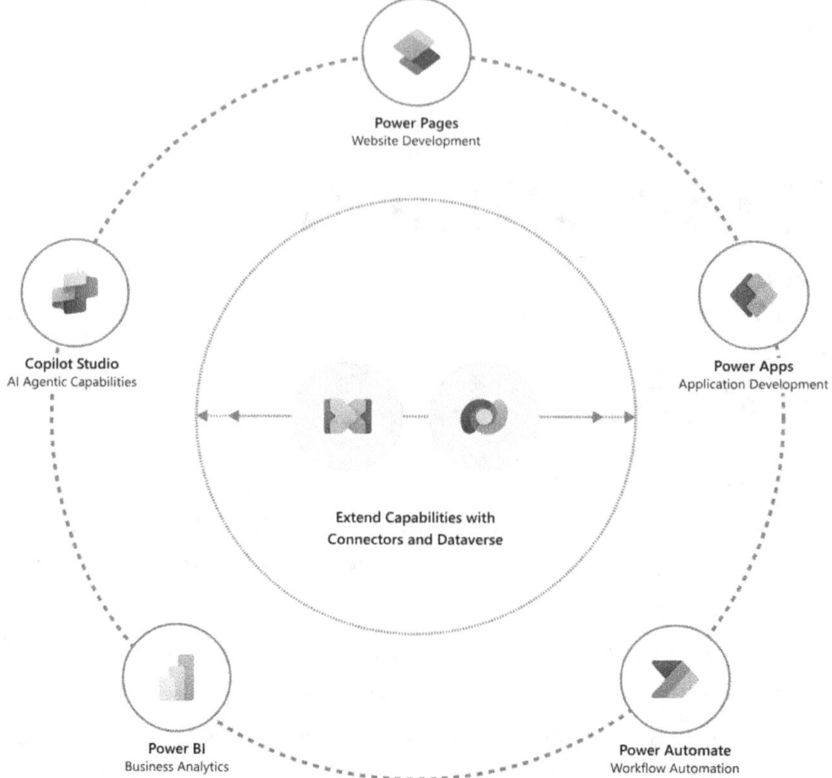

Figure 3-1. *Data Integration in Power Platform*

This chapter introduces the **core data concepts** that every Power Pages builder must understand. You will see how Power Pages connects to Dataverse, how data flows between users and tables, and how the Data workspace simplifies this interaction.

Figure 3-1 illustrates how Power Pages fits within the broader Microsoft Power Platform ecosystem. At the center, Dataverse and connectors act as the common data and integration layer, enabling seamless data sharing and extensibility across services. Power Pages leverages this foundation to build secure, external-facing websites, while integrating closely with Power Apps for application development, Power Automate for workflow automation, and Power BI for business analytics and insights. Copilot Studio enhances the ecosystem by adding AI-driven and agentic capabilities, enabling intelligent interactions and automation across platforms. This unified architecture allows organizations to build end-to-end, data-driven solutions by combining low-code tools with shared data, automation, analytics, and AI capabilities.

You will focus on three key data experiences:

- **Lists**, to display multiple records

- **Basic forms**, to create or edit single records

- **Multistep forms**, to guide users through complex data entry

All examples are explained visually and step by step, so even readers new to Dataverse can follow along confidently.

Understanding Data Integration in Power Pages

At the heart of every meaningful Power Pages site is **data integration**. While pages, layouts, and styling define how a site looks, data integration defines **what the site does**. It enables users to submit information, view records, track requests, and interact with business data in a secure and structured way.

In Power Pages, data integration is built on top of **Microsoft Dataverse**, which acts as the unified data platform behind your site. Instead of connecting directly to databases or APIs, Power Pages works with Dataverse tables, forms, and views, making data-driven websites accessible even to non-developers.

What Data Integration Means in Power Pages

Data integration in Power Pages refers to the process of

- Connecting a website to Dataverse tables

- Displaying data using lists

- Capturing or updating data using forms

- Enforcing security and permissions automatically

From a user's perspective, this looks simple. They fill a form or view a list. Behind the scenes, Power Pages securely communicates with Dataverse, validates permissions, saves data, and returns results to the page.

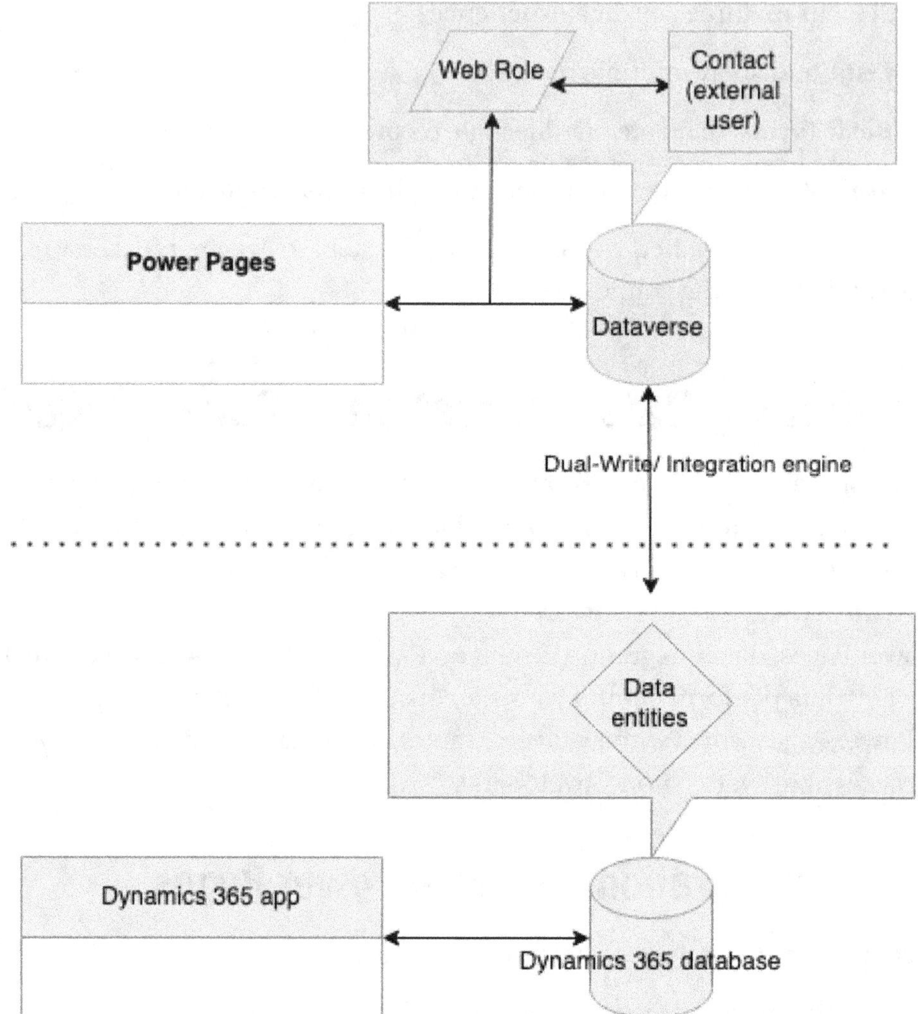

Figure 3-2. *Power Pages Data Access and Security Architecture Using Dataverse*

Figure 3-2 depicts the data integration architecture between Power Pages, Dataverse, and Dynamics 365. Power Pages interacts with Dataverse as the central data platform, where external users are represented as Contacts and access is governed through Web Roles. Dataverse acts as the dual-write and integration engine, synchronizing data between Power Pages and the underlying Dynamics 365 database. Business data is stored as Dataverse entities, which are consumed both by external-facing Power Pages sites and internal Dynamics 365 applications. This architecture ensures secure role-based access for external users, consistent data storage, and seamless data flow between customer-facing websites and internal business applications.

The Role of Microsoft Dataverse

Microsoft Dataverse is the **data backbone** of Power Pages. It stores both

- Business data such as registrations, feedback, applications

- Configuration data such as forms, views, and permissions

Dataverse provides

- Structured tables with relationships

- Built-in validation and data types

- Security through roles and permissions

- Seamless integration with the Power Platform

Because Power Pages and Dataverse are tightly integrated, any data captured through a site is immediately available to Power Apps, Power Automate, and Power BI.

Internal vs. External Data Access

Power Pages is designed primarily for **external-facing scenarios**, but the data itself lives inside your organization's Dataverse environment.

Table 3-1. *Comparison of Internal Users and External Users in Power Pages*

Aspect	Internal Users	External Users
Where data lives	Dataverse	Dataverse
How data is accessed	Apps, automation	Power Pages site
Security model	Dataverse roles	Web roles + table permissions
Typical use	Employees	Customers, partners, citizens

This separation ensures that external users never access Dataverse directly. All interactions flow through the Power Pages runtime, which enforces security rules.

How Data Flows Between Power Pages and Dataverse

Understanding the data flow helps troubleshoot issues and design better experiences.

Step-by-Step Flow:

1. A user opens a page containing a list or form.

2. Power Pages checks authentication and permissions.

3. Dataverse retrieves or accepts data securely.

4. The page renders data or confirms submission.

This entire process is handled by the platform. You do not need to write APIs or server-side code.

Core Data Components in Power Pages

Table 3-2. *Three Main Components Used by Power Pages to Expose Dataverse Data*

Component	Purpose	Typical Scenario
List	Display multiple records	View requests, registrations
Basic Form	Create or edit one record	Contact form, feedback
Multistep Form	Guide complex input	Applications, onboarding

Each component maps directly to Dataverse forms and views, ensuring consistency between internal apps and external sites.

Why Power Pages Uses Forms and Views

Power Pages does not invent a new data model. Instead, it reuses existing Dataverse artifacts.

- **Views** define how records are displayed in lists.

- **Forms** define how records are created or edited.

This approach offers major benefits:

- One data model, multiple experiences

- Consistent validation and formatting

- Less duplication and maintenance

Changes made to forms or views in Dataverse can immediately affect how data appears on the site.

Tip   Think of Dataverse as the single source of truth. Power Pages is simply a secure window into that data.

Common Data Integration Scenarios

Power Pages data integration is commonly used for

- Public registration portals

- Feedback and survey collection

- Support request submission

- Application and approval workflows

- Partner or customer self-service portals

All these scenarios rely on the same underlying pattern. Tables store data, forms capture it, lists display it.

What Data Integration Does Not Cover

It is equally important to understand the boundaries.

Data integration in Power Pages

- Does not bypass security rules

- Does not expose raw databases

- Does not require custom APIs for standard scenarios

Advanced integrations with external systems are possible, but the core focus of this chapter is **Dataverse-based integration**, which covers most real-world use cases.

Data Architecture Overview for Power Pages

Before working with forms and lists, it is important to understand the **data architecture that powers a Power Pages site**. A clear mental model of how data is stored, related, and presented will help you design cleaner solutions, avoid common mistakes, and troubleshoot issues faster.

Power Pages follows a **layered data architecture** built on Microsoft Dataverse. Each layer has a specific responsibility. Together, they enable secure, scalable, and reusable data-driven websites.

High-Level Data Architecture

At a high level, Power Pages data architecture can be viewed as four connected layers:

Tables → Relationships → Forms and Views → Page Components

Each layer builds on the one below it. Pages never talk directly to raw data. Instead, they interact through forms and views, which ensures consistency and security.

Dataverse Tables: The Data Foundation

Dataverse tables are where **all business data is stored**. Every record created through a Power Pages form is saved into a table, and every list retrieves records from a table.

Table 3-3. *Two Types of Tables Commonly Used in Power Pages*

Table Type	Description	Examples
Standard tables	Provided by the platform	Contact, Account
Custom tables	Created by makers	Registration, Feedback

Tables define

- Columns and data types

- Required fields

- Relationships with other tables

Good table design is critical. A poorly designed table leads to confusing forms and unusable lists.

The Special Role of the Contact Table

In Power Pages, **external users are represented by records in the Contact table**. This is a core architectural concept.

- Every authenticated site user maps to a Contact record.

- Submitted data can be linked to the Contact automatically.

- Permissions often use Contact-based relationships.

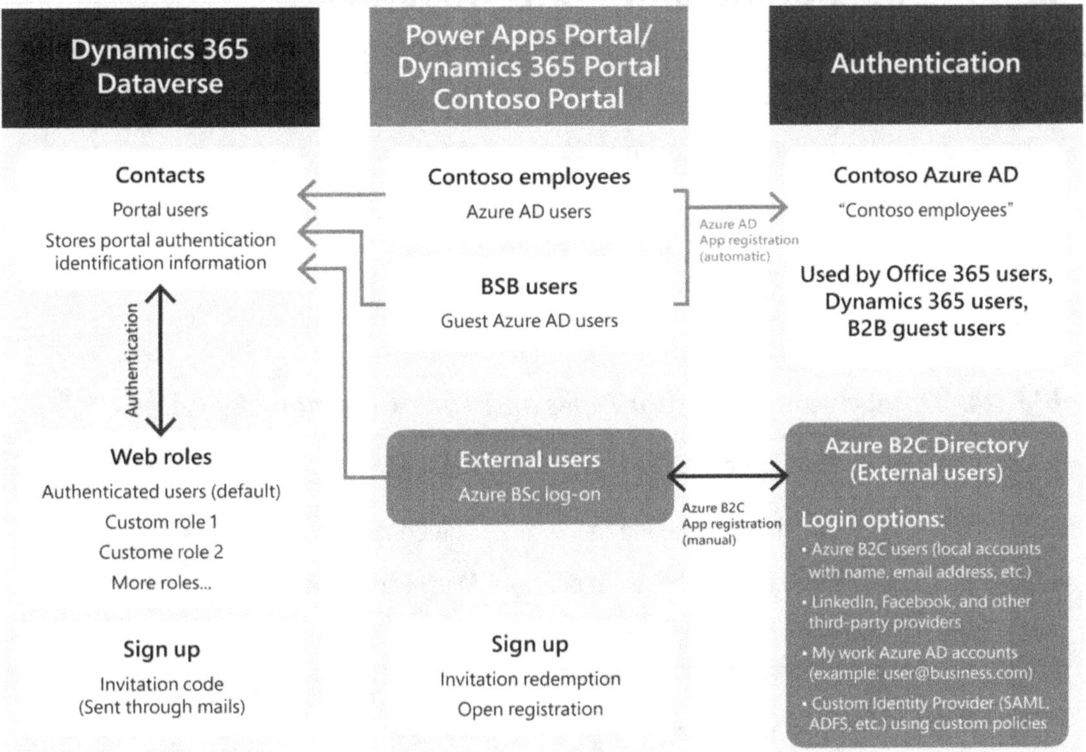

Figure 3-3. *Power Pages Authentication and User Management Architecture with Dataverse, Azure AD, and Azure AD B2C*

Because of this, many custom tables include a lookup column pointing to Contact. This allows each record to be associated with the user who created or owns it.

Figure 3-3 illustrates the authentication and user access model used in Power Pages with Dataverse and Azure Active Directory integrations. Internal users such as Contoso employees authenticate using Azure Active Directory, while business partners and guest users can access the portal through Azure AD B2B. External users authenticate via Azure AD B2C, which supports multiple login options including local accounts, social identities, and custom identity providers. User profile and authentication details are stored as Contact records in Dataverse, and access to portal features is controlled using web roles and permissions. This flexible authentication architecture enables Power Pages to securely support internal, partner, and public users within a single portal experience.

Relationships: Connecting Data Together

Relationships define how tables are connected. They allow Power Pages to show related data and enforce record-level access.

Common relationship patterns include

- Contact → Registration

- Account → Requests

- Contact → Feedback

Table 3-4. *Dataverse Relationship Types and Their Common Use Cases*

Relationship Type	Description	Use Case
One-to-many	One record linked to many	One Contact, many Requests
Many-to-one	Many records linked to one	Many Feedback entries, one Contact
Many-to-many	Records linked both ways	Users and Events

Relationships are essential for

- Filtering lists by user

- Showing only "my records"

- Enabling parent–child data views

Forms: How Data Is Captured and Edited

Forms define **how users create or edit a single record**. Power Pages reuses Dataverse forms rather than inventing new ones.

Forms control

- Which fields appear

- Field order and grouping

- Required fields and validation

Table 3-5. *Form Types and Their Purpose in Power Pages*

Form Type	Purpose	Used In
Main form	Full record editing	Basic forms
Multistep form	Step-by-step input	Applications, onboarding

When a user submits a form on a Power Pages site, the form definition determines how the data is validated and saved.

Views: How Data Is Displayed

Views define **how multiple records are displayed**. Lists in Power Pages are always based on views.

Views control

- Which records appear

- Which columns are visible

- Sorting and filtering

Table 3-6. *View Elements and Their Impact on Lists in Power Pages*

View Element	Impact on Lists
Columns	What users see
Filters	Which records appear
Sort order	Record ordering

By designing views carefully, you control list behavior without touching page design.

Page Data Components. The Presentation Layer

Pages do not work directly with tables. They use **data components** that reference forms and views.

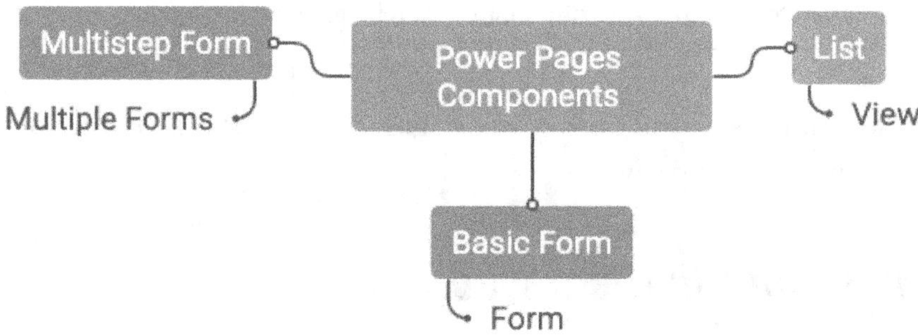

Figure 3-4. *Power Pages Components and Their Functions*

This separation keeps pages clean and reusable. As illustrated in Figure 3-4, Power Pages is built around key data interaction components. Basic Forms are used for single-record data entry and editing, while Multistep Forms support complex scenarios by splitting input across multiple stages. Lists display data using predefined views, enabling users to browse and interact with multiple records efficiently. Together, these components form the core building blocks for creating data-driven experiences in Power Pages.

Why This Architecture Matters

This layered approach provides several advantages:

- One data model supports multiple experiences.

- Changes to forms or views automatically reflect on pages.

- Security is enforced consistently.

- Internal apps and external sites share the same data.

Tip   Design tables and relationships first. Pages and forms are much easier to build when the data model is clear.

Table 3-7. *Common Architecture Mistakes to Avoid*

Mistake	Impact
Designing pages before tables	Rework and confusion
Ignoring relationships	Data not filtering correctly
Overloading one table	Poor performance
Skipping Contact linkage	Hard to secure data

Introduction to the Data Workspace

The **Data workspace** is where Power Pages connects your beautifully designed pages to **real business data**. While the Pages workspace focuses on layout and content, the Data workspace focuses on **tables, forms, views, and how data is exposed to users**. This clear separation helps makers work confidently without mixing design decisions with data modeling tasks.

Think of the Data workspace as the **control room for data integration**. It allows you to see which tables your site uses, create or reuse forms and views, and prepare data components that can later be placed on pages.

What the Data Workspace Is Used For

The Data workspace enables you to

- View Dataverse tables connected to the site

- Create or select **forms** used by Basic Forms and Multistep Forms

- Create or select **views** used by Lists

- Manage how data components are structured before adding them to pages

It does **not** control page layout, navigation, or styling. Its sole purpose is to manage the **data layer** of your Power Pages site.

Data Workspace at a Glance

When you open the Data workspace, you will typically see

- A list of tables used by the site

- Options to create new tables or reuse existing ones

- Access to forms and views associated with those tables

This gives you a centralized view of the site's data model.

Pages Workspace vs. Data Workspace

Understanding the differences between Pages workspace and Data workspace prevents confusion later.

Table 3-8. *Understanding the differences Between Pages Workspace and Data Workspace*

Pages Workspace	Data Workspace
Designs page layout	Manages data structures
Adds sections and components	Creates forms and views
Controls navigation	Controls data presentation
Edits text and media	Defines how data is captured
Focuses on user experience	Focuses on data integrity

Both workspaces are equally important, but they serve very different roles.

How the Data Workspace Fits into the Build Flow

A typical Power Pages build follows the sequence shown in Figure 3-5.

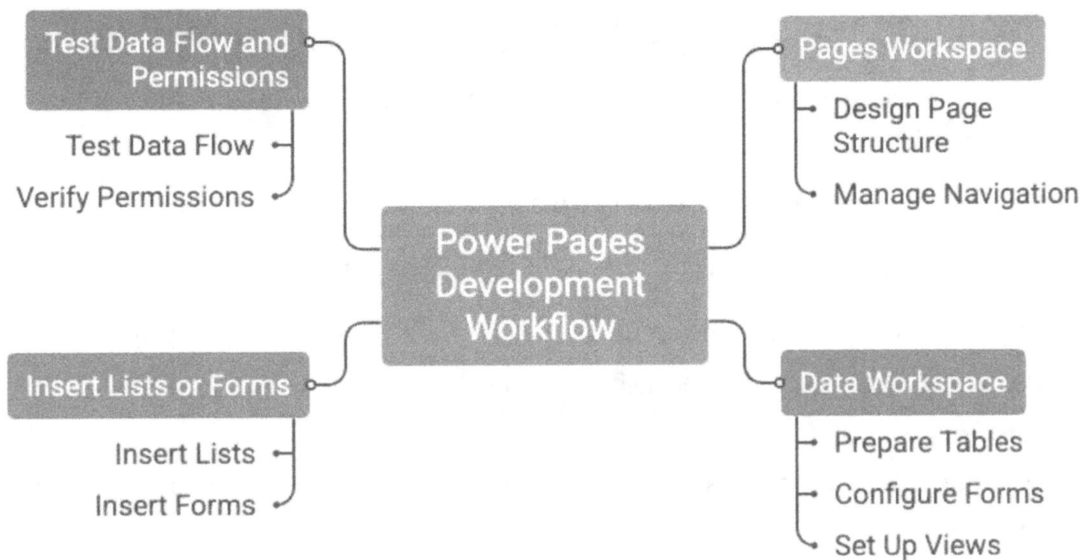

Figure 3-5. *Power Pages Development Workflow*

This approach avoids rework and ensures pages are connected to well-defined data components. As depicted in Figure 3-5, the Power Pages development workflow follows a structured, end-to-end approach. The process begins in the Data workspace, where tables, forms, and views are prepared. Next, the Pages workspace is used to design page structure and manage navigation. Lists and forms are then inserted to enable user interaction with data. Finally, data flow and permissions are tested to ensure secure and accurate access before the site is published.

Working with Tables in the Data Workspace

Tables are the starting point of everything in the Data workspace. From here, you can

- Select standard tables such as Contact or Account

- Create custom tables for your business scenario

- Review columns and relationships

You do not directly place tables on pages. Instead, tables are surfaced through **forms and views**, which are then used by page components.

Forms and Views: The Bridge Between Data and Pages

The Data workspace highlights the importance of **forms** and **views** as **presentation layers.**

Table 3-9. *The Data workspace forms and Views As **Presentation Layers***

Dataverse Artifact	Used For	Appears As
Form	Capturing or editing data	Basic form or Multistep form
View	Displaying multiple records	List

By managing these artifacts centrally, you ensure consistency between internal apps and external websites.

Tip   Create or review forms and views in the Data workspace *before* adding them to pages. This saves time and reduces redesign later.

Why the Data Workspace Is Beginner-Friendly

The Data workspace hides much of the complexity of Dataverse while still giving you control over

- Which fields users see

- How records are filtered

- How data is grouped and ordered

This makes it approachable for business users while still being powerful enough for advanced scenarios.

Table 3-10. *Common Misunderstandings About the Data Workspace*

Misconception	Reality
Data workspace stores data.	Data is stored in Dataverse tables
Lists are created on pages.	Lists are based on views
Forms belong only to pages.	Forms are Dataverse artifacts
Styling happens here.	Styling is handled elsewhere

Clarifying these early avoids confusion as your site grows.

Tip   If data does not appear on a page, check the Data workspace first. Most issues originate from forms, views, or table configuration.

Exploring Tables in the Data Workspace

Tables are the **foundation of all data-driven functionality** in Power Pages. Every form submission, list display, or multistep process ultimately reads from or writes to a Dataverse table. The Data workspace gives you a focused, visual way to explore these tables, understand their structure, and prepare them for use on your site.

In this section, you will learn how to **identify existing tables, understand standard vs. custom tables, and create tables that support real-world Power Pages scenarios.**

Tables in the Context of Power Pages

In Power Pages, you never work with raw databases. Instead, you work with **Dataverse tables**, which provide structure, validation, relationships, and security out of the box.

Each table defines

- What data is stored

- How data is structured through columns

- How records relate to other tables

- How data can be secured and exposed to users

The Data workspace acts as a **window into these tables**, tailored specifically for website builders.

Viewing Tables in the Data Workspace

When you open the Data workspace, you see a list of tables available to your site.

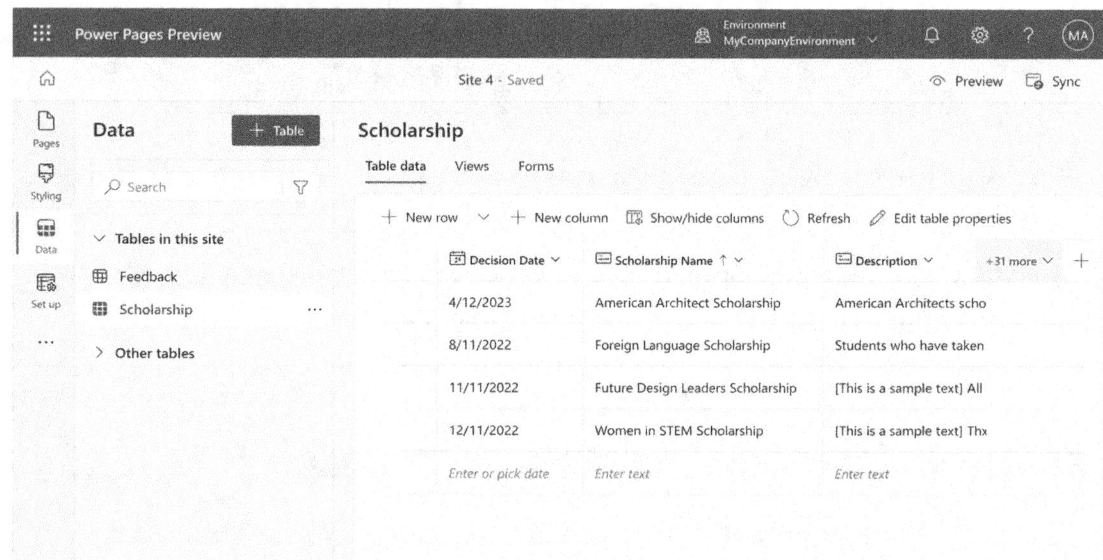

Figure 3-6. *Managing Dataverse Table Data in Power Pages Data Workspace*

As shown in Figure 3-6, the Data workspace in Power Pages allows makers to view and manage Dataverse table records directly within the portal design experience. From this interface, users can add new records, edit existing data, refresh views, and control visible columns. This integrated view simplifies data validation and ensures that tables used in pages, forms, and lists are accurate and up to date before publishing the site.

From here, you can

- Browse tables already used by the site

- Search for specific tables

- Select a table to view its columns, forms, and views

- Create new custom tables when required

This centralized view helps you understand exactly what data your site depends on.

Standard Tables vs. Custom Tables

Dataverse provides many **standard tables** that support common business scenarios. In addition, you can create **custom tables** for site-specific needs.

Table 3-11. *Types of Dataverse Tables and Their Examples in Power Pages*

Table Type	Description	Examples
Standard tables	Built-in, platform-managed	Contact, Account
Custom tables	Created by makers	Registration, Feedback, Requests

Standard tables should be reused whenever they fit your scenario. Custom tables should be created only when you need to store new types of information.

The Importance of the Contact Table

The **Contact table** plays a special role in Power Pages.

- Each authenticated site user maps to a Contact record.

- Data submitted by users is often linked to their Contact.

- Many security rules depend on Contact relationships.

Because of this, most custom tables include a lookup column pointing to Contact. This allows you to associate records with the user who created or owns them.

Exploring Table Columns

Columns define the **shape of the data** stored in a table. When exploring a table, review its columns carefully.

Common column types include

- Text and multiline text

- Number and decimal

- Date and time

- Choice (option set)

- Lookup (relationship to another table)

Good column design improves

- Form usability

- Data validation

- Reporting and automation later

Tip   Name columns clearly and avoid abbreviations. Clear column names make forms easier to understand for users.

Creating a Custom Table from the Data Workspace

When standard tables are not sufficient, you can create a custom table directly from the Data workspace.

Typical steps include

1. Provide a table name and description

2. Choose ownership type

3. Add required columns

4. Save and publish the table

Once created, the table becomes available for forms and lists immediately.

Ownership and Record Association

Table 3-12. *Selecting the Appropriate Ownership Model for Power Pages Is Essential*

Ownership Type	Description	Common Use
User or team owned	Records linked to users	External user submissions
Organization owned	Records shared broadly	Reference data

Most Power Pages scenarios use **user-owned tables** so records can be filtered by the logged-in user.

Relationships Between Tables

Tables rarely exist in isolation. Relationships allow you to

- Filter lists to "my records"

- Display related data

- Enforce record-level access

For example:

- Contact → Feedback

- Contact → Registration

- Account → Requests

Setting up relationships early simplifies form and list configuration later.

Table 3-13. *Common Table Design Mistakes*

Mistake	Impact
Creating too many tables	Unnecessary complexity
Missing Contact lookup	Hard to secure data
Poor column naming	Confusing forms
Ignoring relationships	Lists not filtering correctly

Tip   Design tables with forms and lists in mind. If a field is not needed on a form, reconsider whether it belongs in the table.

Understanding Forms and Views in Dataverse

Once tables are in place, the next layer of Power Pages data integration is **forms and views**. These two Dataverse artifacts act as the **presentation layer** between raw data and your website. Power Pages does not display tables directly. Instead, it uses **views** to show data in lists and **forms** to capture or edit data from users.

Understanding the difference between forms and views, and how Power Pages uses them, is critical for building clean, secure, and user-friendly data experiences.

Why Forms and Views Exist

Dataverse separates data storage from data presentation:

- **Tables** store the data.

- **Forms** define how a single record is edited or viewed.

- **Views** define how multiple records are displayed.

This separation allows the same data to be reused across

- Power Pages websites

- Power Apps (model-driven or canvas apps)

- Power Automate flows

- Power BI reports

Power Pages simply consumes these existing definitions instead of creating new ones.

Forms: How Single Records Are Captured or Edited

A **form** defines how a user interacts with **one record at a time**. When you add a Basic Form or Multistep Form to a page, you are selecting a Dataverse form behind the scenes.

Forms control

- Which fields appear on the page

- Field order and grouping

- Required fields

- Read-only vs. editable fields

- Field-level validation

Table 3-14. *Common Form Types Used in Power Pages*

Form Type	Description	Used For
Main form	Full record create or edit	Basic forms
Multistep form	Step-by-step data capture	Complex scenarios
Read-only form	Display record only	View details pages

In Power Pages, **Main forms** are most commonly used for basic data entry scenarios.

Views: How Multiple Records Are Displayed

A **view** defines how **many records** from a table are shown together. Every list component in Power Pages is based on a Dataverse view.

Views control

- Which records appear

- Which columns are visible

- Sort order

- Filters and conditions

If a record does not appear in a list, the issue is almost always related to the underlying view or permissions.

Table 3-15. *Forms vs. Views—Clear Comparison*

Aspect	Form	View
Record scope	Single record	Multiple records
Used by	Basic form, Multistep form	List
Controls	Fields and layout	Columns and filtering
Validation	Yes	No
Typical action	Create or edit	Display and browse

This distinction helps you choose the right artifact for each scenario.

How Power Pages Uses Forms and Views

Table 3-16. *Power Pages Views and Forms Follow a Consistent Mapping Structure*

Power Pages Component	Uses Dataverse Artifact
Basic Form	Main form
Multistep Form	Multiple forms
List	View

Because of this mapping

- Changing a form affects all pages using it

- Changing a view updates all lists based on it

This makes maintenance easier but also means changes should be made thoughtfully.

Designing Forms for External Users

Forms used in Power Pages should be designed differently from internal forms. Best practices include

- Show only essential fields

- Use clear labels and instructions

- Avoid system or internal-only fields

- Group related fields logically

Tip   If a form feels long, consider using a multistep form instead of adding more fields to a single page.

Designing Views for Lists

Views used in lists should focus on **readability** rather than completeness.

Best practices:

- Limit the number of columns

- Use meaningful column names

- Apply filters to show only relevant records

- Sort records logically

Tip   Create separate views for Power Pages instead of reusing internal app views blindly.

Table 3-17. *Common Mistakes with Forms and Views*

Mistake	Impact
Reusing internal forms	Confusing user experience
Too many fields on a form	Low completion rate
Unfiltered views	Users see unrelated data
Editing forms without testing	Broken page flows

Designing Multistep Forms for Complex Scenarios

Multistep forms are designed for scenarios where collecting all information in a single screen would overwhelm users. In Power Pages, multistep forms break a long or complex process into smaller, logical steps. This improves usability, reduces errors, and increases form completion rates.

This section explains when to use multistep forms, how they work, and how to design them effectively.

What Is a Multistep Form in Power Pages?

A **multistep form** guides users through a sequence of steps. Each step collects a specific set of information and saves progress before moving forward.

Typical characteristics:

- Information is divided into logical stages.

- Users can move forward and backward.

- Data is saved at each step.

- Validation occurs step by step.

Simple Analogy for Readers

Think of a multistep form like a **wizard**.

- **Step 1:** Basic details

- **Step 2:** Additional information

- **Step 3:** Review and submit

Users focus on one task at a time instead of facing a long, intimidating form.

***Table 3-18.** When Should You Use Multistep Forms?*

Scenario	Why Multistep Forms Help
Job applications	Large amount of personal data
Loan or grant requests	Multiple validations and approvals
Event registrations	Optional and conditional steps
Student admissions	Data collected in stages
Service onboarding	Progressive data capture

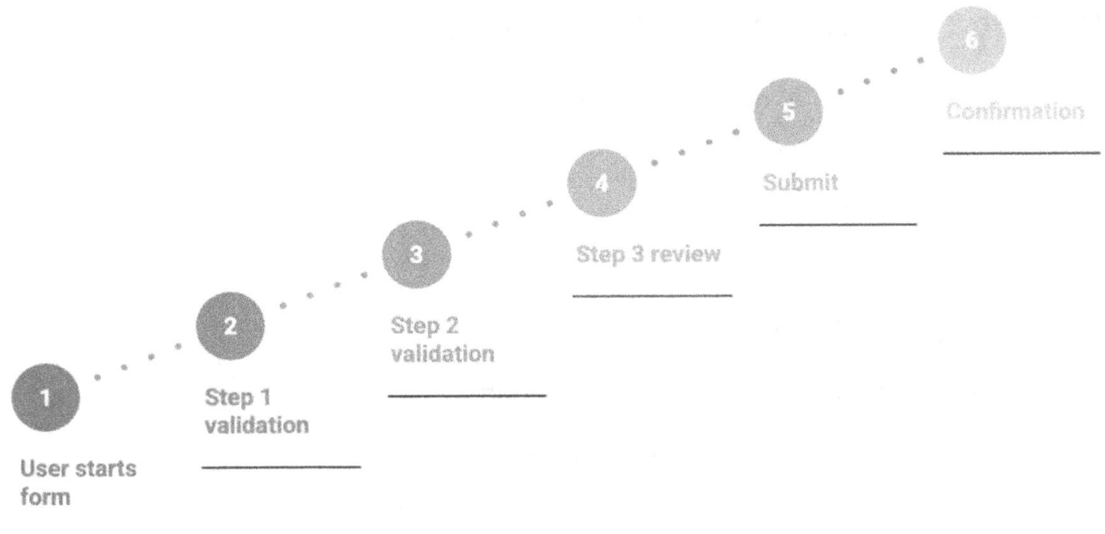

Figure 3-7. *Multistep Form Flow*

As illustrated in Figure 3-7, a multistep form in Power Pages guides users through a structured, sequential flow. The process starts when the user initiates the form, followed by multiple validation steps to ensure data accuracy at each stage. Users are then given an opportunity to review the entered information before submission, and the flow concludes with a confirmation step, providing a clear and user-friendly data entry experience

Designing Steps and Flow

Before building a multistep form, plan the flow on paper or digitally.

A good design follows this pattern:

1. **Introduction or overview**

2. **Primary information**

3. **Supporting or additional details**

4. **Review and confirmation**

Tip   Each step should answer one clear question. If a step feels too long, split it into two.

Mapping Steps to Dataverse Tables

Each step in a multistep form can be connected to

- A single Dataverse table

- Multiple related tables

For example:

- **Step 1:** Applicant details

- **Step 2:** Address and contact information

- **Step 3:** Supporting documents or preferences

This mapping allows Power Pages to save data incrementally and maintain consistency even if users leave and return later.

Navigation and User Feedback

Navigation controls are critical for usability.

Best practices include

- Clear **Next** and **Previous** buttons

- Progress indicators showing current step

- Confirmation messages after submission

Add a multistep form   ✕

Set up   Form name * ⓘ

On submit   Multistep form 1

CAPTCHA
                    Show progress indicator   ⬤
More options
                    Allow multiple entries per person   ⬤

                                              OK   Cancel

Figure 3-8. Adding and Configuring a Multistep Form in Power Pages

As shown in Figure 3-8, Power Pages allows makers to add a multistep form through a simple configuration dialog. During setup, the form name is defined, and options such as displaying a progress indicator and allowing multiple entries per user can be enabled. Additional settings like CAPTCHA and submit behavior help improve security and control user interactions, making multistep forms suitable for structured and repeatable data collection scenario. Avoid unexpected jumps between steps. Users should always feel in control of where they are in the process.

Validation and Error Handling

One major advantage of multistep forms is **step-level validation**.

Benefits:

- Errors are caught early.

- Users fix issues immediately.

- Less frustration at final submission.

Validation messages should be

- Clear and specific

- Placed near the relevant field

- Written in simple language

Tip   Validate only what is required at each step. Avoid blocking progress with unnecessary rules.

Designing for Mobile Users

Multistep forms work especially well on mobile devices because they reduce scrolling. Design considerations:

- Limit the number of fields per step.

- Use clear labels and spacing.

- Test navigation buttons on small screens.

Table 3-19. *Common Design Mistakes to Avoid*

Mistake	Impact
Too many fields in one step	User fatigue
Unclear step titles	Confusion
No progress indicator	Uncertainty
Over-validation	Drop-offs
Mixing unrelated fields	Poor data quality

Real-World Example. Application Form Flow

A typical application form might follow this structure:

- **Step 1:** Personal details

- **Step 2:** Qualifications or requirements

- **Step 3:** Preferences and options

- **Step 4:** Review and submit

This mirrors how users naturally think, making the process feel intuitive.

Test and Validate Data Flow Between the Site and Dataverse

Once pages and forms are designed, the most critical step before publishing is **testing and validating the data flow between your Power Pages site and Dataverse.** This ensures that data entered by users is saved correctly, retrieved accurately, and displayed securely according to permissions. Skipping this step can result in empty forms, missing records, or unintended data exposure.

This section walks through **how data flows, what to test, and how to validate each stage confidently.**

Understanding the Data Flow Lifecycle

At a high level, data flow in Power Pages follows a predictable path:

User action → Site request → Dataverse processing → Site response

Here's what happens behind the scenes:

1. A user submits a form or loads a list on the site.

2. Power Pages sends a secure request to Dataverse.

3. Dataverse validates permissions and processes the request.

4. Data is saved or retrieved.

5. The site displays the result to the user.

Testing ensures each step works as expected.

Step 1: Validate Table and Column Mapping

Before testing the site, confirm that your Dataverse tables are correctly configured.

Checklist:

- Required tables exist

- Columns match the fields used in forms

- Data types are correct (text, choice, date, lookup)

- Relationships are properly defined

Table 3-20. *Key Data Validation Checks for Power Pages Forms*

Item to Verify	Why It Matters
Required columns	Prevents failed submissions
Lookup relationships	Ensures related data loads
Choice values	Avoids invalid selections
Column permissions	Controls data visibility

Tip   If a form loads but does not save data, column configuration is often the first place to check.

Step 2: Test Form Submission from the Site

Forms are the most common interaction point with Dataverse.

Testing steps:

1. Open the page containing the form

2. Enter sample data in all required fields

3. Submit the form

4. Confirm success or confirmation message

Then, switch to Dataverse and verify:

- A new record is created

- Field values match the submitted input

- Timestamps and ownership are correct

Tip Use realistic test data. It helps uncover validation, formatting, and usability issues early.

Step 3: Validate List Retrieval and Display

Lists display data from Dataverse back to users. Testing lists confirms read access and filtering logic.

Things to test:

- Does the list load for authenticated users

- Are the correct records displayed

- Are filters and sorting applied correctly

- Are related fields (lookups) shown as expected

Table 3-21. *Common List Issues and Their Likely Causes in Power Pages*

Issue	Likely Cause
Empty list	Missing table permissions
Partial data	Scope set incorrectly
Wrong records	Incorrect filter logic
Errors on load	Relationship misconfiguration

Step 4: Verify Table Permissions and Security

Data flow is always subject to **table permissions**. Even if a page is visible, data will not load unless permissions allow it.

Validation steps:

- Confirm the correct web role is assigned

- Check permission scope (Global, Contact, Parent)

- Ensure Create, Read, and Write rights are correct

Tip   If a form loads but submission fails silently, permission scope is often the issue.

Step 5: Test with Different User Scenarios

Always test with **multiple user types**, not just admin access.

Test as

- Anonymous user

- Authenticated user

- User with limited web role

- User with elevated access

Table 3-22. *User Roles and Access Validation Scenarios in Power Pages*

User Type	What to Validate
Anonymous	Page visibility only
Authenticated	Data creation and viewing
Restricted role	Limited record access
Admin role	Full data access

This ensures least-privilege access works as intended.

Step 6: Validate Multistep and Partial Saves

For multistep forms, test

- Navigation between steps

- Data persistence between steps

- Resume behavior after page refresh

Ensure

- Data from earlier steps is saved correctly

- Validation errors appear at the right step

- Users can continue without losing progress

Step 7: Monitor Errors and Logs

If issues occur

- Review Dataverse records for partial saves

- Check browser console for errors

- Validate configuration changes were synced

Common causes of failure include

- Missing permissions

- Required fields not exposed on the form

- Incorrect table relationships

Tip   After making changes in advanced configuration tools, always sync before retesting.

Table 3-23. *Common Data Flow Issues and Fixes*

Problem	Root Cause	Fix
Form submits but no record created	Missing Create permission	Update table permissions
List shows no records	Scope too restrictive	Adjust permission scope
Fields not saving	Column mismatch	Update form mapping
Users see too much data	Over-permissive scope	Apply least privilege

Apply Best Practices for Clean, Scalable Data Design

Clean and scalable data design is the foundation of every successful Power Pages solution. A well-designed data model ensures that your site performs efficiently, remains secure, and can grow as business requirements evolve. Poor data design, on the other hand, leads to slow performance, complex maintenance, and security risks.

This section outlines **practical best practices** to help you design Dataverse data models that are easy to understand, reuse, and scale over time.

Why Data Design Matters in Power Pages

Power Pages sites are tightly coupled with Microsoft Dataverse. Every form submission, list view, and multistep process depends on how well your tables, columns, and relationships are designed.

Good data design helps you

- Improve site performance

- Simplify security configuration

- Reduce rework when requirements change

- Support multiple sites or apps using the same data

Think in Business Entities, Not Pages

Start by identifying **business entities**, not website pages.

For example:

- Use *Application, Registration,* or *Feedback* as tables

- Avoid creating tables named after pages like *ContactUsPageData*

This approach ensures your data model remains reusable across:

- Multiple pages

- Multiple sites

- Power Apps and Power Automate flows

Tip   If the data makes sense outside the website, your table name is probably correct.

Design Tables with a Clear Purpose

Table 3-24. *Each Dataverse Table Should Represent a Single Clear Concept*

Good Practice	Avoid
One table per business entity	One table for everything
Clear, descriptive names	Vague or generic names
Reusable across apps	Page-specific tables

Use Relationships Instead of Duplicating Data

Avoid storing the same data in multiple tables. Instead, use **relationships**.

For example:

- A *Customer* table linked to many *Requests*

- An *Application* linked to multiple *Documents*

Benefits:

- Data consistency

- Easier updates

- Better reporting and filtering

Tip   If you find yourself copying the same fields into multiple tables, a relationship is probably missing.

Choose Column Types Carefully

Dataverse provides many column types. Choosing the right one improves validation and performance.

Table 3-25. *Common Dataverse Column Types and Their Recommended Usage*

Column Type	Best Use
Text	Names, descriptions
Choice	Status, category
Date	Birthdate, submission date
Lookup	Relationships
Yes/No	Flags and approvals

Avoid using plain text where structured types are available.

Tip   Use Choice columns instead of free-text fields to improve consistency and filtering.

Normalize First, Then Simplify

A scalable design usually starts **normalized**, then simplifies only when necessary. Good normalization:

- Keeps tables focused
- Reduces duplication
- Improves long-term scalability

However, avoid over-normalization that makes forms overly complex. Strike a balance based on real usage.

Plan for Security from Day One

Security in Power Pages depends on **table permissions**, which rely on clean data design. Best practices:

- Use a *Contact* or *Account* relationship for ownership
- Design tables with permission scopes in mind
- Avoid exposing sensitive data in shared tables

Table 3-26. *Security-Focused Design Choices and Their Benefits in Power Pages*

Design Choice	Security Benefit
Clear ownership relationships	Easier row-level security
Separate sensitive tables	Reduced exposure
Least-privilege access	Better compliance

Tip   If you cannot clearly explain who should see a table's data, redesign the table.

Design for Multistep Forms and Future Growth

If you expect complex processes

- Break data into logical tables

- Design steps around data groups

- Allow partial saves where possible

This makes it easier to

- Add new steps later

- Reuse data in other apps

- Support reporting and automation

Naming Conventions and Consistency

Consistent naming improves readability and maintenance.

Best practices:

- Use singular table names

- Avoid abbreviations

- Use consistent prefixes if required

- Keep display names user-friendly

Example:

- **Table Name:** *Application*

- **Column Name:** s

Table 3-27. *Avoid Common Data Design Mistakes*

Mistake	Impact
Page-based table design	Poor reuse
Too many required fields	User drop-off
No relationships	Data duplication
Overly broad permissions	Security risks
Hard-coded logic in pages	Low scalability

Validate and Refine Continuously

Data design is not a one-time task.

After testing

- Review how users interact with forms

- Monitor performance of lists

- Adjust relationships and columns if needed

Use feedback and real usage patterns to refine your model.

Chapter Summary

- This chapter transforms Power Pages sites from visually appealing pages into fully **data-driven websites** by introducing data integration with Microsoft Dataverse.

- Readers learn how Power Pages securely connects to Dataverse, enabling external users to **store, view, and interact with business data** through lists, basic forms, and multistep forms.

- The chapter explains the **core data architecture** of Power Pages, covering tables, relationships, forms, views, and page components, and how each layer builds on the one below.

- Microsoft Dataverse is presented as the **single source of truth**, storing both business data and configuration, while enforcing validation, relationships, and security automatically.

- The **Data workspace** is introduced as the control center for data integration, clearly separated from page design, and used to manage tables, forms, and views before exposing them on pages.

- Readers gain a practical understanding of **standard vs. custom tables**, the special role of the **Contact table**, and how relationships enable record ownership, filtering, and secure access.

- The chapter details how **forms capture or edit single records**, how **views control list behavior**, and how Power Pages reuses these Dataverse artifacts for consistency and maintainability.

- Multistep forms are covered as a best practice for **complex data entry scenarios**, improving usability through step-by-step input, validation, progress indicators, and partial saves.

- A structured approach to **testing and validating data flow** is provided, ensuring data is saved correctly, retrieved accurately, and protected through table permissions and web roles.

- The chapter emphasizes **clean, scalable data design**, encouraging readers to think in business entities, design relationships early, plan for security, and avoid common data modeling mistakes.

- By the end of this chapter, readers can confidently design, connect, test, and secure Dataverse-backed data experiences in Power Pages.

- This chapter lays the foundation for advanced scenarios in later chapters, including automation, analytics, and enterprise-scale solutions built on reliable, well-designed data models.

CHAPTER 4

Advanced Customization and Developer Extension

Chapter Objectives

The objective of this chapter is to help readers move beyond the limitations of low-code development in Power Pages and explore advanced customization techniques using professional developer tools.

By the end of this chapter, readers will be able to

- Understand when and why to extend Power Pages using pro-developer approaches

- Use Liquid to create dynamic, data-driven content

- Design reusable and scalable layouts using Web Templates

- Implement the Portals Web API for real-time data interaction

- Build custom UI components using the Power Apps Component Framework (PCF)

- Integrate Power Automate Cloud Flows to automate business processes

- Apply advanced configuration techniques to improve performance and security

- Design and implement real-world, enterprise-grade portal solutions

© Dr. Gomathi S, Jerald Felix 2026
Dr. Gomathi S and J. Felix, *Getting Started with Microsoft Power Pages*,
https://doi.org/10.1007/979-8-8688-2667-2_4

This chapter equips readers with the knowledge required to transform Power Pages from a low-code platform into a **fully customizable and extensible web application framework**.

Moving Beyond Low-Code: When and Why to Extend

Microsoft Power Pages is designed to empower makers to build secure and scalable websites with minimal coding. Using the design studio, site templates, and built-in components, many business scenarios can be implemented quickly without writing any code.

However, as organizations scale their solutions, they often encounter scenarios where **low-code capabilities alone are not sufficient**. At this stage, developers may need to introduce **advanced customization techniques** to meet specific functional or architectural requirements.

Some common situations where advanced customization becomes necessary include

- Displaying dynamic data in a custom layout

- Integrating with external APIs

- Implementing complex business logic

- Building reusable UI components

- Creating highly personalized user experiences

By combining the low-code capabilities of Power Pages with developer tools such as **Liquid templates, Web Templates, Portals Web API, and Code Components**, developers can create powerful enterprise-grade web applications.

Table 4-1. *Common Scenarios Requiring Developer Extensions*

Scenario	Description	Recommended Approach
Dynamic content rendering	Display user-specific information	Liquid templates
External system integration	Connect with external REST APIs	Portals Web API
Custom UI elements	Interactive components not available by default	Code Components (PCF)
Advanced workflows	Automate backend processes	Power Automate
Complex page layouts	Fully customized page structure	Web Templates

These capabilities allow organizations to **maintain the simplicity of low-code development while introducing the flexibility of professional development practices**.

Tip   Before jumping into advanced customization, always evaluate whether the requirement can be solved using out-of-the-box features. Over-engineering early can increase complexity and maintenance effort. Use pro-dev tools only when there is a clear business or technical need.

Professional Developer Tools and Methods

While Power Pages provides a powerful visual designer for makers, developers have access to additional tools that allow deeper customization and control over the website structure.

These tools enable developers to implement **advanced UI customization, data integration, and automation capabilities** beyond the visual editor.

The most commonly used developer tools in Power Pages include

- Liquid Templates

- Web Templates

- Portals Web API

- Power Apps Component Framework (PCF)

- Power Automate Cloud Flows

- Power Platform CLI

Each tool plays a specific role in extending the functionality of the portal.

Table 4-2. *Key Developer Tools in Power Pages*

Tool	Purpose	Typical Use Case
Liquid	Dynamic server-side rendering	Display Dataverse records
Web Templates	Custom HTML page layouts	Build reusable UI structures
Portals Web API	Client-side data operations	Create or update records
Code Components (PCF)	Custom UI components	Advanced interactive controls
Power Automate	Process automation	Notifications, approvals
Power Platform CLI	DevOps and deployment	CI/CD for portals

Developers typically work with these tools through the **Portal Management App** or external development environments like **Visual Studio Code**.

Developer Workflow in Power Pages

The typical workflow for developers working with Power Pages involves the following steps:

1. Configure the portal structure using the **Design Studio**

2. Use **Web Templates and Liquid** to customize page layouts

3. Implement **Portals Web API** for dynamic data interaction

4. Extend UI capabilities using **PCF code components**

5. Automate backend processes using **Power Automate**

6. Deploy and manage changes using **Power Platform CLI**

This hybrid approach allows teams to combine **low-code productivity with full developer control**, making Power Pages suitable for both rapid prototyping and enterprise-grade solutions.

Mastering Liquid for Dynamic Content

Liquid is a **server-side templating language** used in Microsoft Power Pages to dynamically render content from Dataverse and personalize the user experience. It allows developers to insert logic into web pages, making it possible to display records, control layout behavior, and tailor content based on the logged-in user.

Unlike traditional server-side programming languages, Liquid is designed to be **secure and controlled**, meaning it cannot execute arbitrary code. Instead, it provides predefined objects, filters, and tags that allow developers to safely interact with portal data.

By mastering Liquid, developers can build **data-driven web pages that adapt dynamically to the user and the data stored in Dataverse**.

Understanding How Liquid Works in Power Pages

When a user loads a page in Power Pages, the server processes any Liquid code embedded within the page before sending the final HTML to the browser. This means the dynamic content is generated **on the server side**, ensuring better performance and improved security.

Liquid typically interacts with the following components within Power Pages:

- Dataverse tables

- Web pages

- Web roles

- Site settings

- User profile information

Liquid code is usually written inside

- Web Templates

- Content Snippets

- Web Page Copy fields

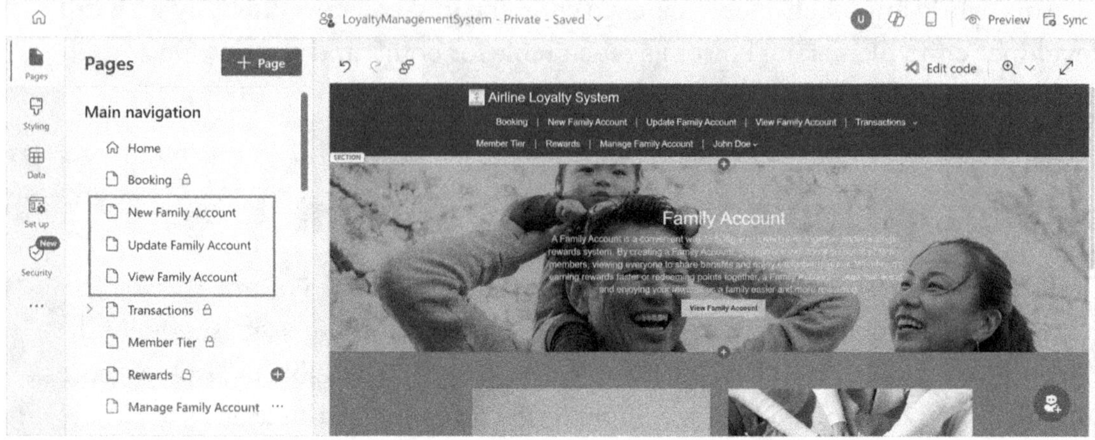

Figure 4-1. *Editing Liquid Templates Within the Power Pages Portal Management Application*

Core Components of Liquid

Liquid syntax is composed of three main building blocks that help developers control how data is displayed.

Table 4-3. *These Elements, Including Liquid and Components, Enable Developers to Build Dynamic Pages That Respond to Different Conditions*

Component	Description	Example
Objects	Represent data available in the portal	{{ user.fullname }}
Tags	Used for logic and control flow	{% if user %}
Filters	Modify or format output	`{{ name

Displaying User Information

One of the simplest uses of Liquid is displaying information about the currently authenticated user.

Example

```
{% if user %}
Welcome, {{ user.fullname }}!
{% else %}
Welcome, Guest!
{% endif %}
```

This snippet checks whether a user is logged in. If the user is authenticated, the page displays their name. Otherwise, it shows a generic greeting.

Accessing Dataverse Records

Liquid can retrieve and display data stored in Dataverse tables. This enables developers to create dynamic lists, dashboards, or custom content sections.

Example: Displaying Records from a Table

```
{% fetchxml contacts %}
<fetch>
  <entity name="contact">
    <attribute name="fullname"/>
    <attribute name="emailaddress1"/>
  </entity>
</fetch>
{% endfetchxml %}

<ul>
{% for contact in contacts.results.entities %}
  <li>{{ contact.fullname }} - {{ contact.emailaddress1 }}</li>
{% endfor %}
</ul>
```

In this example:

- FetchXML retrieves contact records from Dataverse

- A loop iterates through the results

- Each record is rendered dynamically on the page

Conditional Logic in Liquid

Liquid allows developers to control how content is displayed based on conditions.

Example

```
{% assign user_roles = user.roles %}
{% if user.roles contains 'Administrators' %}
<p>You have administrative access.</p>
{% else %}
 <p>You are a standard user.</p>
 {% endif %}
```

This enables role-based personalization of portal content.

Using Loops to Render Lists

Loops are commonly used to display multiple records retrieved from Dataverse.

Example

```
<ul>
{% for record in entityview.records %}
<li>{{ record.name }}</li>
{% endfor %}
</ul>
```

This approach is useful when rendering

- Product catalogs

- Service requests

- Event listings

- Knowledge articles

Useful Liquid Filters

Filters help format and transform output before displaying it on the page.

Table 4-4. *Liquid Filters Make It Easier to Present Data in a User-Friendly Format*

Filter	Purpose	Example
Upcase	Convert text to uppercase	`{{ name
Downcase	Convert text to lowercase	`{{ name
Date	Format date values	`{{ createdon
Truncate	Shorten long text	`{{ description

Personalizing Portal Content

Liquid can be used to customize content based on user context, including

- Login status

- User roles

- User profile data

- Table records

For example, organizations can display different dashboard sections depending on whether the user is a **customer, partner, or internal staff member**.

This capability makes Power Pages ideal for building **secure self-service portals** where each user sees only the information relevant to them.

Best Practices for Using Liquid

To maintain performance and maintainability, developers should follow a few recommended practices when using Liquid in Power Pages. Following these practices ensures the portal remains **fast, secure, and scalable**.

Table 4-5. *Best Practices for Using Liquid in Power Pages*

Best Practice	Explanation
Minimize complex queries	Avoid retrieving unnecessary records
Use caching where possible	Improves page performance
Keep templates modular	Reuse templates across multiple pages
Follow security guidelines	Respect table permissions

Building and Managing Web Templates

Web Templates are a foundational concept in Power Pages that allow developers to define **custom page structures using HTML, CSS, and Liquid.** While Liquid enables dynamic data rendering, Web Templates provide the **layout and structure** in which that data is presented.

In simple terms, if Liquid is the logic, Web Templates are the **skeleton of your web pages**.

They are especially useful when you want to

- Create reusable layouts across multiple pages

- Standardize UI design across the portal

- Embed dynamic content using Liquid

- Build fully customized page experiences

Understanding Web Templates

A Web Template is a reusable block of HTML and Liquid code that can be applied to one or more web pages. These templates are stored and managed in the **Portal Management App**.

Each Web Template typically contains

- HTML structure

- Liquid logic

- References to CSS and JavaScript

- Dynamic placeholders for content

Tip   Design once, reuse everywhere.

Structure your Web Templates in a modular way with reusable components like headers, footers, and navigation. This not only ensures UI consistency but also reduces long-term maintenance effort when updates are required.

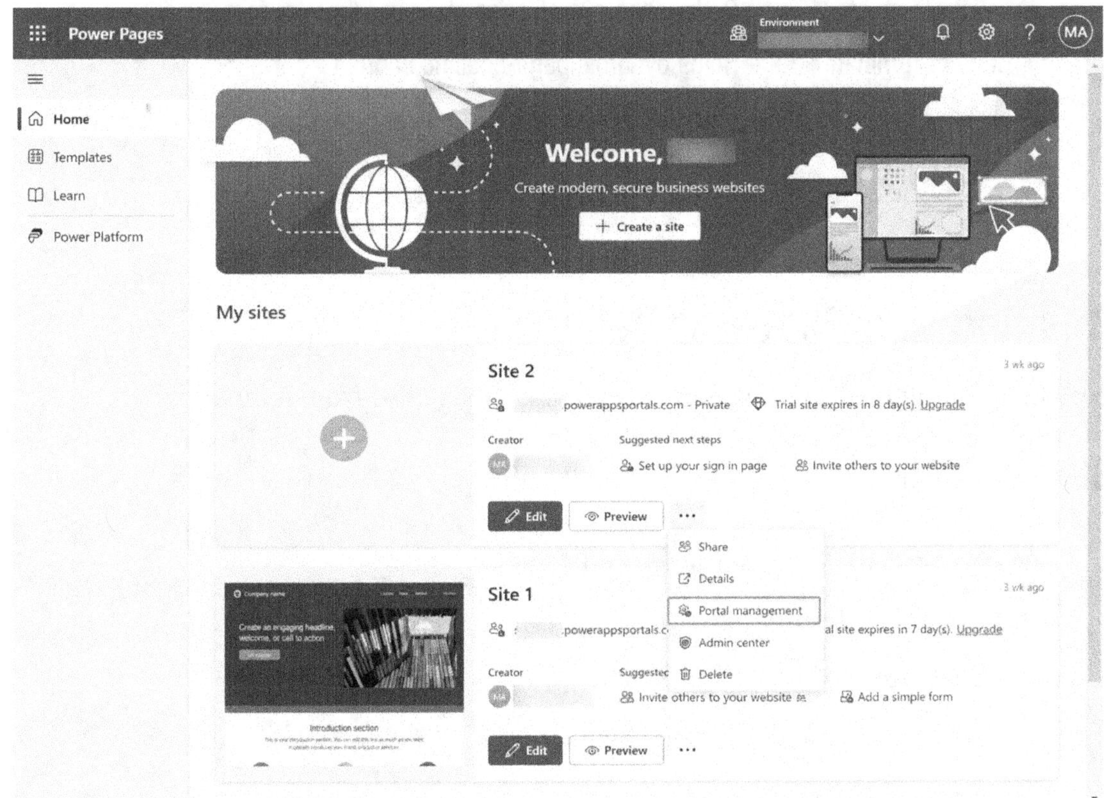

Figure 4-2. *Creating and Managing Web Templates in the Portal Management App*

Web Template Architecture

Web Templates often follow a layered architecture to promote reusability and maintainability.

Key Components

Table 4-6. *Key Components of Web Template Architecture*

Component	Description
Layout Template	Defines the overall page structure (header, footer)
Content Template	Holds dynamic page-specific content
Includes	Reusable partial components
Liquid Logic	Handles dynamic rendering

Creating Your First Web Template

Let's walk through a simple example of creating a reusable layout template.

Step by Step

1. Navigate to **Portal Management App**

2. Go to **Web Templates**

3. Click **New**

4. Provide a name (e.g., Main Layout)

5. Add HTML + Liquid code

6. Save and associate it with a Web Page

Example: Basic Layout Template

```
<!DOCTYPE html>
<html>
```

```
<head>
    <title>{{ page.title }}</title>
</head>
<body>

<header>
    <h1>My Power Pages Site</h1>
</header>

<main>
    {% include 'Page Content' %}
</main>

<footer>
    <p>© 2026 My Company</p>
</footer>

</body>
</html>
```

This template defines a consistent structure with

- Header

- Dynamic content section

- Footer

Using Template Inheritance

One of the powerful features of Web Templates is **template inheritance**, which allows you to create a base layout and extend it across multiple pages.

Example Structure

Table 4-7. *Example of Web Template Structure and Usage*

Template Name	Purpose
Base Layout	Common structure (header/footer)
Home Template	Homepage-specific design
Dashboard Template	User-specific content

This approach ensures

- Consistency across pages
- Easier maintenance
- Reduced duplication

Embedding Liquid Inside Web Templates

Web Templates become truly powerful when combined with Liquid.

Example: Dynamic Content Rendering

```
<h2>Welcome, {{ user.fullname }}</h2>

{% if user %}
<p>Your recent activities:</p>

<ul>
{% for record in user.activities %}
<li>{{ record.name }}</li>
{% endfor %}
</ul>

{% endif %}
```

This allows developers to build **personalized dashboards and user-specific experiences**.

Reusable Components Using Includes

To avoid repeating code, developers can create reusable components and include them in multiple templates.

Example

```
{% include 'Navbar' %}
{% include 'Sidebar' %}
{% include 'Footer' %}
```

This modular approach improves

- Code readability

- Maintainability

- Development speed

Best Practices for Web Templates

To ensure your templates are scalable and efficient, follow these best practices:

Table 4-8. *Best Practices for Designing Web Templates*

Best Practice	Explanation
Keep templates modular	Break into smaller reusable components
Avoid heavy logic in UI	Move complex logic to Liquid where possible
Use consistent naming	Improves maintainability
Optimize performance	Minimize unnecessary data rendering
Test across devices	Ensure responsive design

Real-World Enterprise Scenarios

Web Templates are widely used in enterprise implementations of Power Pages.

Scenario 1: Customer Self-Service Portal

A company builds a support portal where users can

- View tickets

- Submit requests

- Track status

Web Templates ensure consistent UI across all pages.

Scenario 2: Partner Portal

Organizations create partner portals with

- Role-based dashboards

- Sales insights

- Document sharing

Templates enable dynamic layouts based on partner roles.

Scenario 3: Employee Portal

Internal portals use templates to display

- HR data

- Announcements

- Internal tools

Templates help maintain branding and structure.

Implementing the Portals Web API

The **Portals Web API** is one of the most powerful features available to developers in Power Pages. It enables client-side scripts (typically JavaScript) to interact directly with Dataverse data from within the portal.

With the Web API, developers can perform **Create, Read, Update, and Delete (CRUD)** operations without relying entirely on server-side rendering through Liquid. This makes it ideal for building **interactive, real-time user experiences**.

Understanding the Portals Web API

The Portals Web API is a REST-based interface that allows secure communication between the portal frontend and Dataverse.

It is typically used when

- You need real-time data updates without page reload

- You want to build interactive forms or dashboards

- You need to integrate custom JavaScript logic

- You want to perform background operations

Tip   Always configure Table Permissions and limit field access before enabling the Web API. Never expose unnecessary tables or sensitive fields, as the API directly interacts with your Dataverse data.

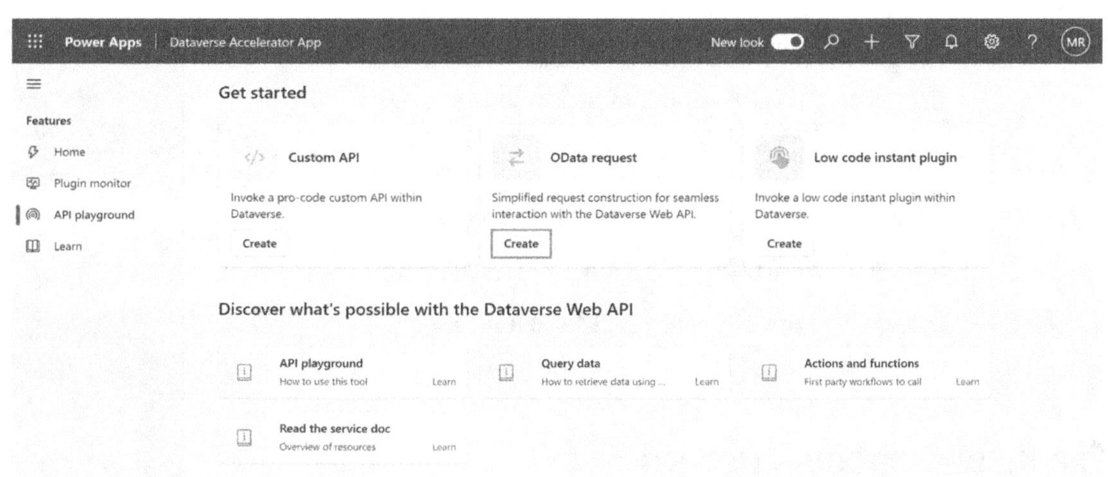

Figure 4-3. *Inspecting Web API Calls in the Browser Developer Tools*

Enabling the Portals Web API

Before using the Web API, it must be enabled through **Site Settings** in the Portal Management App.

Required Site Settings

Table 4-9. Required Site Settings for Enabling Portals Web API

Setting Name	Value	Purpose
Webapi/<table>/enabled	true	Enables API access for a table
Webapi/<table>/fields	*	Defines accessible fields
Webapi/error/innererror	true	Enables detailed error messages

Replace <table> with the logical name of your Dataverse table (e.g., contact, account).

Performing CRUD Operations

The Web API allows full CRUD operations using standard HTTP methods.

Table 4-10. CRUD Operations Using Portals Web API

Operation	HTTP Method	Description
Create	POST	Create a new record
Read	GET	Retrieve records
Update	PATCH	Modify existing record
Delete	DELETE	Remove a record

Example: Creating a Record

```
fetch("/_api/contacts", {
  method: "POST",
  headers: {
    "Content-Type": "application/json"
  },
  body: JSON.stringify({
    firstname: "Jerald",
```

```
    lastname: "Felix"
  })
})
.then(response => response.json())
.then(data => console.log(data));
```

This creates a new contact record in Dataverse.

Example: Retrieving Records

```
fetch("/_api/contacts?$select=fullname,emailaddress1")
  .then(response => response.json())
  .then(data => {
    data.value.forEach(contact => {
      console.log(contact.fullname);
    });
  });
```

This fetches and displays contact details dynamically.

Example: Updating a Record

```
fetch("/_api/contacts(<record-id>)", {
  method: "PATCH",
  headers: {
    "Content-Type": "application/json"
  },
  body: JSON.stringify({
    firstname: "Updated Name"
  })
});
```

Example: Deleting a Record

```
fetch("/_api/contacts(<record-id>)", {
  method: "DELETE"
});
```

Authentication and Security

Security is a critical aspect of the Portals Web API. Unlike traditional APIs, access is governed by **Power Pages security model**, not just API keys.

Key Security Concepts

Table 4-11. *Key Security Concepts in Portals Web API*

Concept	Description
Table Permissions	Controls access to Dataverse tables
Web Roles	Defines user access levels
Column Permissions	Restricts access to specific columns within a Dataverse table
Authentication	Ensures only logged-in users access data

The Web API automatically respects these permissions, ensuring that users can only access data they are authorized to see.

Handling Errors and Responses

When working with APIs, handling responses properly is essential.

Example

```
fetch("/_api/contacts")
  .then(response => {
    if (!response.ok) {
      throw new Error("API error");
    }
    return response.json();
  })
  .then(data => console.log(data))
  .catch(error => console.error(error));
```

Real-World Use Cases

Scenario 1: Dynamic Form Submission

Instead of page reload, users submit forms, and data is saved instantly using API calls.

Scenario 2: Live Dashboard

Data updates in real-time without refreshing the page.

Scenario 3: External Integration

Portal interacts with external systems using JavaScript and API calls.

Utilizing Code Components (PCF)

As Power Pages evolves into a powerful platform for building enterprise-grade applications, there are scenarios where standard components and templates are not sufficient. This is where **Code Components**, built using the **Power Apps Component Framework (PCF)**, come into play.

PCF allows developers to create **custom, reusable UI components** using modern web technologies such as **TypeScript, HTML, and CSS**, and integrate them seamlessly into Power Pages.

These components enable highly interactive, rich user experiences that go beyond the default capabilities of the platform.

Understanding PCF in Power Pages

The Power Apps Component Framework (PCF) provides a structured way to build custom controls that can interact with Dataverse data and respond to user input dynamically.

PCF components are typically used when

- You need advanced UI elements (e.g., custom charts, maps)

- You want reusable components across multiple pages

- Default controls do not meet business requirements

- You need real-time interactivity

PCF Architecture Overview

A PCF control consists of several key parts that define its behavior and structure.

Table 4-12. *Core Components of a PCF Control*

Component	Description
Manifest (ControlManifest.Input.xml)	Defines properties, inputs, and configuration
Index.ts	Main logic of the component
CSS	Styling for the component
HTML (Virtual DOM)	UI rendering
Context	Provides data and environment information

PCF Lifecycle

Each PCF component follows a lifecycle that determines how it is initialized, updated, and destroyed.

Table 4-13. *PCF Lifecycle Methods*

Method	Purpose
init	Initializes the component
updateView	Updates UI when data changes
getOutputs	Returns values to Dataverse
destroy	Cleans up resources

Understanding this lifecycle is critical for building efficient and responsive components.

Creating a PCF Component

Developers typically create PCF components using the **Power Platform CLI** and **Visual Studio Code**.

Step by Step

1. Install Power Platform CLI

2. Create a new PCF project

3. Define properties in the manifest file

4. Write component logic in TypeScript

5. Build and test locally

6. Deploy to Power Platform

Example: Basic PCF Control Logic

```
public updateView(context: ComponentFramework.Context<IInputs>): void {
    const value = context.parameters.sampleProperty.raw || "Default Value";
    this.container.innerHTML = `<div>${value}</div>`;
}
```

This simple example renders dynamic data inside a custom UI element.

Using PCF in Power Pages

Once deployed, PCF components can be integrated into Power Pages through

- Forms (model-driven forms exposed in portal)

- Custom pages

- Embedded components in templates

These components can interact with

- Dataverse data

- User input

- External APIs

Advantages of Using PCF

Table 4-14. *PCF Advantage*

Advantage	Description
Reusability	Build once, use across multiple pages
Rich UI	Create modern, interactive components
Performance	Efficient rendering using framework lifecycle
Flexibility	Full control over behavior and design

Best Practices for PCF Development

Table 4-15. *PCF Development*

Best Practice	Explanation
Keep components lightweight	Avoid unnecessary complexity
Optimize rendering	Use efficient update logic
Follow naming conventions	Maintain consistency
Secure data access	Respect Dataverse permissions
Test thoroughly	Ensure cross-browser compatibility

Real-World Use Cases

Scenario 1: Interactive Dashboard

Custom chart components displaying real-time data from Dataverse.

Scenario 2: Map Integration

Embedding location-based services using external APIs.

Scenario 3: Advanced Form Controls

Custom input fields like rating systems, sliders, or multi-select visuals.

Configuring Power Automate Cloud Flows in Your Site

Power Pages becomes significantly more powerful when integrated with **Power Automate Cloud Flows**. While Liquid and Web API handle data rendering and interaction, Power Automate enables you to **automate business processes, trigger actions, and connect with external systems**.

This integration allows your portal to move beyond being just a website into a **fully automated business solution**.

Understanding Power Automate Integration

Power Automate allows you to create workflows (flows) that are triggered by events such as

- Form submissions

- Button clicks

- Record creation or updates

- HTTP requests from the portal

These flows can then perform actions like

- Sending emails

- Updating Dataverse records

- Calling external APIs

- Creating approvals

Types of Flows Used with Power Pages

Power Automate supports different types of flows depending on how they are triggered.

Table 4-16. *Types of Power Automate Flows*

Flow Type	Description	Use Case
Automated Flow	Triggered by events (e.g., record creation)	Send notifications
Instant Flow	Triggered manually or via button/API	User-triggered actions
Scheduled Flow	Runs at defined intervals	Data synchronization
HTTP-triggered Flow	Triggered via API call	Portal integration

Triggering Flows from Power Pages

One of the most common approaches is to trigger a flow using an **HTTP request** from the portal.

Step by Step

1. Create a flow in Power Automate

2. Select trigger: **When an HTTP request is received**

3. Define JSON schema for input

4. Add required actions (e.g., send email)

5. Save the flow and copy the HTTP URL

6. Call the flow from Power Pages using JavaScript

Tip   Avoid building overly complex flows for simple tasks. Break large workflows into smaller, reusable flows to improve performance, debugging, and maintainability.

Example: Calling a Flow from Power Pages

```
fetch("https://prod-xx.logic.azure.com/workflows/your-flow-url", {
  method: "POST",
```

```
headers: {
  "Content-Type": "application/json"
},
body: JSON.stringify({
  name: "Jerald",
  issue: "Support request"
})
})
.then(response => response.json())
.then(data => console.log(data));
```

This example sends data from the portal to a Power Automate flow.

Example Scenario: Support Ticket Notification

Let's consider a real-world scenario:

When a user submits a request in the portal and the system cannot resolve it, a flow is triggered to **notify the support team via email.**

Flow Design

1. **Trigger**: HTTP request

2. **Action**: Parse JSON

3. **Action**: Send email

4. **Action**: Log record in Dataverse

Table 4-17. *Example Flow Actions*

Step	Action	Purpose
1	HTTP Trigger	Receive data from portal
2	Parse JSON	Extract input fields
3	Send Email	Notify support team
4	Create Record	Store request in Dataverse

Passing Data from Power Pages

Data passed from the portal can include

- User name

- Email

- Form inputs

- Record IDs

This allows flows to act contextually based on user actions.

Security Considerations

When exposing flows via HTTP endpoints, security becomes critical.

Table 4-18. *Security Best Practices*

Practice	Description
Use secure URLs	Keep flow URL confidential
Validate input	Prevent malformed data
Use authentication	Add API keys or tokens if needed
Limit exposure	Avoid public misuse

Combining Power Automate with Other Tools

Power Automate works best when combined with other Power Pages capabilities:

- **Liquid**: Display dynamic content

- **Web API:** Perform real-time operations

- **PCF:** Enhance UI interactions

- **Power Automate:** Handle backend workflows

This combination creates a **complete end-to-end solution**.

Real-World Use Cases

Scenario 1: Escalation Workflow

If a chatbot or portal cannot resolve a query, automatically escalate to L2 support.

Scenario 2: Approval Process

Users submit requests that trigger approval workflows.

Scenario 3: Notification System

Send SMS or email alerts based on user actions.

Advanced Configuration and Optimization

As Power Pages solutions grow in complexity and scale, it becomes essential to focus on **advanced configuration, performance tuning, and security optimization**. While earlier sections focused on building features, this section ensures your solution is **efficient, secure, and enterprise-ready**.

A well-configured portal not only improves user experience but also ensures **scalability, maintainability, and compliance with organizational standards**.

Understanding Advanced Configuration

Advanced configuration in Power Pages involves fine-tuning various platform settings and components, including

- Site Settings

- Security (Web Roles and Table Permissions)

- Caching mechanisms

- Performance optimization techniques

- Monitoring and debugging tools

These configurations help control how your portal behaves under different conditions and user loads.

Site Settings Deep Dive

Site Settings are key-value pairs used to control portal behavior dynamically without modifying code.

Table 4-19. *Common Site Settings in Power Pages*

Setting	Purpose
Authentication/Registration/Enabled	Enable or disable user registration
Search/Enabled	Enable global search
Webapi/<table>/enabled	Enable Web API access
Portal/EnableCustomErrors	Control error visibility
Cache/Enabled	Enable caching

These settings allow developers to **quickly modify portal behavior without redeployment**.

Security Configuration

Security is a critical aspect of any Power Pages implementation. The platform uses a layered security model.

Table 4-20. *Security Components in Power Pages*

Component	Description
Web Roles	Define user roles
Table Permissions	Control access to data
Column Permissions	Restrict field-level access
Authentication Providers	Manage login mechanisms

Proper configuration ensures that users can only access **authorized data and features**.

Performance Optimization Techniques

Optimizing performance is essential for delivering a smooth user experience, especially under heavy load.

Key Techniques

- Enable caching to reduce server load

- Minimize API calls and data retrieval

- Optimize Liquid queries

- Use pagination for large datasets

- Reduce unnecessary scripts and styles

Table 4-21. *Performance Optimization Strategies*

Strategy	Benefit
Caching	Faster page load times
Efficient queries	Reduced server processing
Lazy loading	Improved initial load performance
Minified assets	Reduced bandwidth usage
CDN usage	Faster content delivery

Caching in Power Pages

Caching plays a significant role in improving performance. It allows frequently accessed data to be stored temporarily, reducing repeated processing.

Types of caching include

- Server-side caching

- Output caching

- Data caching

Proper caching configuration can dramatically improve **response time and scalability**.

Debugging and Monitoring

To maintain a stable portal, developers must actively monitor and debug issues.

Common Debugging Techniques

- Enable detailed error messages (for development only)
- Use browser developer tools
- Monitor network/API calls
- Analyze logs and telemetry

Table 4-22. Debugging and Monitoring Tools

Tool	Purpose
Browser DevTools	Inspect requests and UI
Power Platform Admin Center	Monitor environment health
Application Insights	Track performance and errors
Portal Diagnostics	Identify configuration issues

Governance and Maintainability

Enterprise-grade solutions require proper governance practices.

Key Practices

- Use consistent naming conventions
- Maintain documentation

- Use solution-based deployments

- Implement version control

- Follow ALM (Application Lifecycle Management)

Real-World Optimization Scenario

Scenario: High-Traffic Customer Portal

An organization experiences slow performance due to increased traffic.

Optimization Steps

1. Enable caching

2. Optimize Liquid queries

3. Reduce API calls

4. Implement CDN for static assets

5. Monitor using Application Insights

Result: Improved load times and better user experience.

Real-World Extension Scenarios

After exploring the full range of developer capabilities in Power Pages, it is important to understand how these concepts come together in **real-world implementations**. In enterprise environments, solutions are rarely built using a single feature. Instead, they combine **Liquid, Web Templates, Web API, PCF components, and Power Automate** to deliver complete, business-ready applications.

This section highlights practical scenarios where advanced customization transforms Power Pages into a **powerful digital platform**.

Scenario 1: Customer Self-Service Portal

Organizations often build portals that allow customers to resolve issues independently without contacting support.

Key Features

- View and track support tickets

- Submit new service requests

- Access knowledge base articles

- Personalized dashboard

Technologies Used

Table 4-23. *Technologies Used in Customer Self-Service Portal Implementation*

Component	Purpose
Liquid	Display customer-specific data
Web Templates	Structured UI layout
Web API	Real-time ticket updates
Power Automate	Email notifications
Security (Web Roles)	Restrict access to user data

Scenario 2: Partner Collaboration Portal

A partner portal allows external business partners to collaborate, access data, and manage operations securely.

Key Features

- Partner-specific dashboards

- Sales and performance insights

- Document sharing

- Role-based access

Technologies Used

Table 4-24. *Technologies Used in Partner Collaboration Portal Implementation*

Component	Purpose
Web Templates	Custom partner UI
Liquid	Role-based rendering
Web API	Data interaction
PCF	Interactive dashboards
Table Permissions	Secure data access

Scenario 3: Employee Service Portal

Internal portals streamline employee processes and improve productivity.

Key Features

- Leave management
- HR requests
- Internal announcements
- Document access

Technologies Used

Table 4-25. *Technologies Used in Employee Service Portal Implementation*

Component	Purpose
Power Automate	Approval workflows
Liquid	Personalized content
Web Templates	Consistent layout
Dataverse	Data storage
Security Roles	Controlled access

Scenario 4: Real-Time Dashboard Application

Organizations require dashboards that display live data without refreshing the page.

Key Features

- Live metrics and KPIs
- Interactive charts
- Data filtering
- Auto-refresh

Technologies Used

Table 4-26. *Technologies Used in Real-Time Dashboard Implementation*

Component	Purpose
Web API	Real-time data fetch
PCF	Custom chart components
JavaScript	Dynamic UI updates
Liquid	Initial rendering

Scenario 5: External System Integration Portal

Many organizations need to integrate Power Pages with external systems such as ERP, CRM, or third-party APIs.

Key Features

- Data synchronization

- External API integration

- Automated workflows

- Cross-platform communication

Technologies Used

Table 4-27. *Technologies Used for External System Integration*

Component	Purpose
Web API	Send/receive data
Power Automate	Integration workflows
JavaScript	API calls
Site Settings	Configuration management

End-to-End Architecture Overview

In real-world scenarios, all components work together as a unified architecture.

Table 4-28. *End-to-End Solution Architecture*

Layer	Technology	Purpose
Presentation Layer	Web Templates, Liquid	UI and rendering
Interaction Layer	JavaScript, Web API	User interaction
Component Layer	PCF	Custom UI elements
Automation Layer	Power Automate	Business workflows
Data Layer	Dataverse	Data storage
Security Layer	Web Roles, Permissions	Access control

Key Takeaways from Real-World Implementations

- Combine multiple tools for best results
- Design with scalability in mind
- Prioritize security at every layer
- Optimize performance early
- Use modular and reusable components

Tip   Instead of designing features in isolation, always visualize the complete solution architecture. Combining Liquid, Web API, PCF, and Power Automate effectively is what differentiates a basic portal from an enterprise-grade solution.

Best Practices Across Scenarios

Table 4-29. *Best Practices for Real-World Power Pages Implementations*

Best Practice	Explanation
Use layered architecture	Improves maintainability
Keep UI and logic separate	Enhances flexibility
Reuse components	Reduces development effort
Monitor performance	Ensures reliability
Implement strong security	Protects sensitive data

Chapter Summary

- This chapter transforms Power Pages from a low-code website builder into a fully extensible platform by introducing advanced customization techniques and professional developer tools.

- Readers learn how to go beyond out-of-the-box capabilities and extend portal functionality using Liquid, Web Templates, the Portals Web API, Code Components, and Power Automate.

- The chapter explains the transition from maker-based development to a hybrid approach where developers enhance flexibility, control, and scalability without losing the benefits of low-code.

- Liquid is introduced as the foundation for dynamic content rendering, enabling personalized, data-driven experiences by securely accessing Dataverse data within the portal.

- Web Templates are presented as the structural backbone of the portal, allowing developers to design reusable layouts, enforce UI consistency, and embed dynamic logic using Liquid.

- The Portals Web API is explored as a key enabler for real-time interaction, allowing client-side operations such as create, read, update, and delete without requiring full page reloads.

- Code Components using the Power Apps Component Framework are introduced to build rich, interactive, and reusable UI elements that extend beyond standard portal capabilities.

- Power Automate integration is explained as a way to connect the portal with automated workflows, enabling business processes such as notifications, approvals, and external integrations.

- The chapter covers advanced configuration techniques including site settings, security models, caching, and performance optimization to ensure solutions are secure, efficient, and scalable.

- Readers gain insight into debugging, monitoring, and governance practices that help maintain enterprise-grade solutions in real-world environments.

- Through real-world extension scenarios, the chapter demonstrates how multiple technologies work together to build customer portals, partner systems, employee solutions, and integrated applications.

- The chapter emphasizes a layered architectural approach, encouraging developers to combine presentation, interaction, automation, and data layers effectively.

- By the end of this chapter, readers can confidently design and implement advanced, scalable, and secure Power Pages solutions using professional development techniques.

- This chapter lays the foundation for building enterprise-grade applications and prepares readers for deeper integrations, automation strategies, and complex solution architectures in subsequent chapters.

Security, Deployment, and Administration

Chapter Objectives

A Power Pages site is only as good as the controls that protect it and the processes that keep it running reliably. Design and data integration attract most of the attention during a build, but security, deployment discipline, and ongoing administration are what determine whether a site succeeds in production.

This chapter moves beyond the build phase and takes you through everything you need to lock down, launch, and maintain a Power Pages solution. You will start by understanding the layered security model that governs who can visit a site, what they can see, and what data they can touch. From there, you will configure real authentication providers, Microsoft Entra External ID, OAuth 2.0 social logins, and local accounts, and then use web roles and table permissions to apply granular access controls to Dataverse data.

The second half of the chapter shifts to operations. You will work through a structured go-live checklist, learn how to move site configurations between environments using Application Lifecycle Management (ALM) practices, and explore the Power Pages admin center for monitoring and maintenance. The chapter closes with practical guidance on diagnosing the most common deployment problems so that you can resolve issues quickly rather than spending hours searching for answers.

By the end of this chapter, you will be able to configure a production-ready, securely authenticated Power Pages site, manage it through its full lifecycle, and troubleshoot problems with confidence.

© Dr. Gomathi S, Jerald Felix 2026
Dr. Gomathi S and J. Felix, *Getting Started with Microsoft Power Pages*,
https://doi.org/10.1007/979-8-8688-2667-2_5

Understanding Power Pages Security

Security in Power Pages is not a single switch you flip before going live. It is a set of overlapping controls that work together to protect your site at every layer. Understanding how those layers interact is the foundation for every configuration decision you will make in this chapter.

The Layered Security Model

Think of Power Pages security as three concentric rings. The outermost ring controls whether a visitor can reach the site at all, this is authentication. The middle ring determines what pages, lists, and forms that visitor can access; this is page and web role authorization. The innermost ring governs which rows and columns of Dataverse data the visitor can read, create, update, or delete, this is table and column permission security.

Each ring must be deliberately configured. Leaving any one of them open exposes more than you intend. Table 5-1 summarizes each security layer, what it controls, and where it is configured.

***Table 5-1.** Power Pages Security Layers*

Security Layer	What It Controls	Where It Is Configured
Authentication	Who can sign in and which identity providers are accepted	Authentication settings in the Power Pages admin center
Web Roles	Which site pages, lists, and forms a signed-in contact can access	Portal Management app or Power Pages Security workspace
Table Permissions	Which Dataverse records a contact can read, create, update, or delete	Portal Management app or Power Pages Security workspace
Column Permissions	Which individual columns within a table a contact can view or modify	Portal Management app, Column Permissions tab
Page Permissions	Whether a page is visible to anonymous or specific web roles only	Power Pages Design Studio, Page settings

Role-Based Access and Authentication Models

Power Pages uses a contact-centric model for authenticated users. When someone signs in, the platform looks for a Contact record in Dataverse that matches their identity. That Contact is then assigned one or more web roles, and it is those web roles, not the identity provider, that define what the person can do on the site.

This separation is intentional. It means you can change identity providers without rewriting your permission model, and you can assign the same web role to contacts who signed in through completely different authentication methods.

Anonymous Users

Any visitor who lands on your site without signing in is treated as an anonymous user. Power Pages assigns this visitor a built-in web role called Anonymous Users automatically. This role has very limited permissions by default, typically read access to public pages only. You should never grant anonymous users write access to Dataverse tables unless there is a specific, well-considered business reason for doing so.

Authenticated Users

Once a visitor signs in successfully, they become an authenticated user. Power Pages automatically assigns them the built-in Authenticated Users web role in addition to any custom web roles you have configured for that contact. The Authenticated Users role acts as a baseline, giving every signed-in contact a minimum level of access that you can then extend with more specific roles.

Custom Web Roles

Beyond the two built-in roles, you can create as many custom web roles as your solution requires. A partner portal, for example, might have roles such as Partner Admin, Partner Member, and Read-Only Partner. Each role carries its own set of page permissions and table permissions, giving you precise control over what different groups of contacts can see and do.

Key principle: Always apply the principle of least privilege. Start with no permissions and add only what each role genuinely needs. It is far easier to grant additional access later than to discover that a role has been silently reading data it should never have seen.

Authentication Setup

Power Pages supports a range of authentication providers out of the box, from enterprise identity platforms such as Azure Active Directory B2C and Microsoft Entra ID to social OAuth providers like Google and LinkedIn, and even simple local accounts where contacts register directly on the site with an email address and password. Choosing the right provider, or combination of providers, depends on who your users are and how your organization manages identity. Table 5-2 compares each provider type, its ideal use case, and the key considerations to keep in mind.

Table 5-2. *Power Pages Authentication Provider Comparison*

Provider Type	Best Suited For	Key Consideration
Azure AD B2C	External customers, partners, large scale, branded sign-in	Requires an Azure subscription; more setup but highly customizable
Microsoft Entra ID (Azure AD)	Internal employees signing into partner or supplier portals	Works seamlessly within Microsoft 365 tenants
OAuth 2.0 / OpenID Connect	Social logins, Google, Facebook, LinkedIn, and others	Suitable where social identity is acceptable; lower trust assurance
Local Authentication	Sites where users self-register with email and password	Easiest to set up; credentials stored in Dataverse, requires a strong password policy
SAML 2.0	Enterprise SSO with third-party identity providers	Ideal for organizations with an on-premise IdP or legacy SAML systems

Configuring Azure AD B2C

Azure Active Directory B2C is the recommended choice when you are building a public-facing site for external customers. It handles sign-up, sign-in, password reset, and profile editing through customizable user journeys, and it scales to millions of users without additional infrastructure on your part.

Step by Step: Registering a Power Pages Application in Azure AD B2C

1. **Create an Azure AD B2C Tenant:** In the Azure Portal, navigate to Azure Active Directory B2C and create a new tenant if one does not already exist for your organization. Note the tenant name (e.g., contosob2c.onmicrosoft.com).

2. **Register a New Application:** Inside your B2C tenant, go to App registrations and click New registration. Give the application a meaningful name such as Power Pages Portal. Set the Supported account types to Accounts in any identity provider or organizational directory.

3. **Set the Redirect URI:** Under the Redirect URI section, select Web and enter the callback URL in this format: `https://yoursite.powerappsportals.com/signin-azure-ad-b2c`. Replace yoursite with your actual site subdomain.

4. **Note the Application (Client) ID:** Once the app is registered, copy the Application (client) ID from the Overview blade. You will need this in the next steps.

5. **Create a Client Secret:** Navigate to Certificates and secrets, then New client secret. Choose an expiry period, 12 or 24 months is common, and copy the Value immediately, as it will not be shown again.

6. **Create User Flows:** In your B2C tenant, go to User flows and click New user flow. Create at minimum a sign-up and sign-in flow. Note the flow policy name, for example, B2C_1_susi.

7. **Configure the Provider in Power Pages:** Open your site in Power Pages Studio, navigate to Security then Identity Providers. Choose Azure Active Directory B2C. Enter your B2C tenant name, the Client ID, the Client Secret, the user flow name, and the authority URL.

8. **Test the Sign-In Flow:** Preview your site, click Sign in, and confirm that the B2C hosted sign-in page appears and that a successful login returns the user to your site with a matched Contact record in Dataverse.

Configuring OAuth 2.0 Social Providers

OAuth 2.0 social providers let users sign in with an identity they already trust, a Google account, for example, without you having to manage passwords. The setup pattern is broadly the same for all social providers.

Step by Step: Adding Google As an OAuth Provider

1. **Create OAuth Credentials in Google Cloud Console:** Navigate to console.cloud.google.com, create a project, and under APIs and Services then Credentials, create an OAuth 2.0 Client ID. Set the application type to Web application.

2. **Set the Authorized Redirect URI:** Add `https://yoursite.powerappsportals.com/signin-google` as an authorized redirect URI.

3. **Copy the Client ID and Client Secret** from the Google Console.

4. **In Power Pages Studio,** navigate to Security then Identity Providers then Add provider. Choose Google from the provider list. Enter the Client ID, Client Secret, and accept the default scopes.

5. **Map Claims to Contact Fields:** Power Pages will attempt to match the email returned by Google to an existing Contact's email address. If no match is found, a new Contact can be created automatically, control this behavior via the Authentication/Registration/Enabled site setting.

6. **Test and Verify** by signing in with a Google account and confirming that the Contact record in Dataverse is created or matched correctly.

Configuring Local Authentication

Local authentication stores user credentials directly against the Contact record in Dataverse. It is the quickest provider to configure and works well for internal pilot sites or scenarios where social and enterprise identity providers are not appropriate.

To enable local authentication, no external app registration is required. In Power Pages Studio, navigate to Security then Identity Providers, ensure Local Sign-in is enabled, it is on by default for new sites, and configure the following site settings to control the experience:

- **Authentication/Registration/Enabled:** Set to true to allow new contacts to self-register.

- **Authentication/Registration/RequiresConfirmation:** Set to true to send a confirmation email before activating the account.

- **Authentication/UserManager/PasswordRequiredLength:** Minimum password length. Set to at least 10 for production sites.

- **Authentication/UserManager/PasswordRequireNonAlphanumeric:** Set to true to require at least one special character.

- **Authentication/LoginTrackingEnabled:** Set to true to log sign-in activity to Dataverse for audit purposes.

Important   Local authentication is convenient but carries more risk than federated identity because your portal now stores credential information. Ensure that password policies are strict, that email confirmation is enabled, and that you have a plan for handling compromised accounts before going live.

Web Roles and Table Permissions

Web roles and table permissions are the heart of Power Pages authorization. Web roles define groups of users, and table permissions define exactly what data those groups can see and interact with. Together they form a matrix that you can tune with precision, right down to individual columns on a Dataverse table.

Creating Web Roles

Web roles are created and managed in the Portal Management model-driven app or directly in the Security workspace of the Power Pages Design Studio.

Step by Step: Creating a Custom Web Role

1. **Open the Portal Management App:** From make.powerpages. microsoft.com, select your site, choose the more options menu, and open the Portal Management app.

2. **Navigate to Security then Web Roles.** Click New.

3. **Enter a name** for the role, for example, Partner Manager. Add a description so future administrators understand what the role is for.

4. **Set Authenticated Users Role to No** unless this role should automatically apply to every signed-in user. For custom roles you almost always leave this as No.

5. **Set Anonymous Users Role to No** unless this role should apply to every unauthenticated visitor.

6. **Save the Record:** Your new web role now exists but has no permissions attached yet.

7. **Associate the Role with Contacts:** Open the Contact record for a user, navigate to the Web Roles subgrid, and add the new role. Contacts can hold multiple web roles simultaneously.

Configuring Table Permissions

Table permissions attach to web roles and define what CRUD operations that role can perform against a specific Dataverse table. The scope setting is particularly important, it controls how broadly the permission applies. Table 5-3 describes each available scope type, what it means in practice, and the typical scenario in which it is used.

Table 5-3. *Table Permission Scope Types*

Scope	What It Means	Typical Use Case
Global	The role can see all records in the table regardless of ownership	Admin or internal staff roles that need full visibility
Contact	The role can only see records where a specific lookup column points to the signed-in contact	A customer viewing only their own orders or cases
Account	The role can see records associated with the contact's parent account	A company employee seeing all records for their employer
Parent	The role can access child records of a parent record it already has permission to see	Viewing line items that belong to an approved order
Self	Applied to the Contact table, the contact can only read and update their own contact record	Self-service profile pages

Step by Step: Creating Table Permissions

1. **In the Portal Management app,** navigate to Security then Table Permissions and click New.

2. **Enter a name** that clearly identifies what this permission controls, for example, Customer, Read Own Cases.

3. **Select the Table Name:** Choose the Dataverse table this permission applies to, for example, the Case table.

4. **Select the Website** this permission belongs to.

5. **Set the Access Type:** Choose the appropriate CRUD permissions, Read, Write, Create, Delete, Append, Append To. Tick only what is genuinely needed.

6. **Set the Scope:** For a customer viewing their own cases, choose Contact and select the lookup column on the Case table that links back to the Contact.

7. **Associate with a Web Role:** In the Web Roles subgrid on the Table Permission record, add the web role that should receive this permission.

8. **Save:** Repeat for each combination of table, scope, and web role that your solution requires.

Column Permissions

Column permissions add a further level of control below table permissions. Even if a web role has Read access to a table, you can restrict which individual columns of that table are visible. This is valuable when a table contains sensitive fields, such as a credit limit, internal notes, or a cost price, that should not be exposed to external users even though they need to see other fields on the same record.

- **Column permissions require a parent table permission**, they cannot exist alone.

- **You can set Read, Write, or both** on any given column.

- **If a column has no column permission record**, it inherits the access level from the parent table permission.

- **Use column permissions on tables that mix public and sensitive fields**, such as the Contact table where you want users to update their own name and email but not their credit limit.

Tip   After configuring any web role or table permission change, test by opening a private browser window and signing in as a contact with that specific web role. Always verify both what the user can see and what they cannot. Configuration mistakes here are among the most common causes of data exposure incidents on live sites.

Data Security Best Practices

Configuring roles and permissions correctly is necessary, but it is not sufficient on its own. A truly secure Power Pages site is one where security thinking is woven into every design decision, from the tables you create in Dataverse to the columns you expose in forms and lists.

Protecting Dataverse Tables and Columns

Restrict Column Exposure in Forms and Lists

Every column you add to a form or list on your Power Pages site is a potential data exposure point. Before adding any column, ask whether the user genuinely needs to see or edit that value. Internal tracking fields, workflow flags, cost fields, and audit columns should almost never appear on an external portal. Removing them from the form layout is a good first step, but it is not sufficient, a determined user with knowledge of the Web API could still query those fields. Add column permissions to fully block access at the data layer.

Enable the Table Permission Security Boundary

By default, anonymous users cannot read from Dataverse tables through the Web API unless you explicitly grant them a table permission. Never disable this boundary. The site setting Webapi/{tableName}/enabled should only be set to true for tables you have deliberately chosen to expose, and only after you have configured the appropriate table permissions for those tables.

Use Dataverse Business Rules for Server-Side Validation

Client-side validation in forms is useful for the user experience, but it can be bypassed. Any data integrity rule that matters for security or compliance, such as preventing a contact from setting their account status to Active without approval, should be enforced using a Dataverse business rule or a server-side Power Automate flow. This way, even if a user manipulates the form, the rule will still fire at the database layer.

Audit Web Role Assignments Regularly

Web role assignments drift over time. Contacts accumulate elevated roles during testing and pilot phases, and those assignments are not always cleaned up before go-live. Build a habit of reviewing role assignments periodically, at least quarterly for production sites, and remove any roles that are no longer justified.

Apply Data Loss Prevention Policies

The Power Platform Admin Center includes Data Loss Prevention (DLP) policy controls that affect Power Pages. Administrators can use these policies to block anonymous access to Dataverse table data at a tenant level, independent of individual site configurations. If your organization's governance requirements prohibit anonymous data access, enforce this at the DLP layer as a safety net alongside your site-level permissions. Table 5-4 brings together the key data security best practices covered in this section, the reasoning behind each one, and how to implement them.

Table 5-4. *Data Security Best Practices for Power Pages*

Best Practice	Why It Matters	How to Implement
Remove sensitive columns from forms and lists	Limits exposure even if table permissions are misconfigured	Edit form columns in Design Studio; add column permissions in the Portal Management app
Use Contact scope for customer data	Ensures users only see their own records	Set Scope to Contact on table permissions with the correct lookup column
Enable email confirmation for local auth	Prevents account creation with fake email addresses	Set Authentication/Registration/ RequiresConfirmation to true in site settings
Enforce DLP policies at tenant level	Provides a governance backstop against misconfigured sites	Configure in the Power Platform Admin Center under Data policies
Use HTTPS only with custom domain and SSL	Encrypts data in transit between user and site	Configure the custom domain and SSL certificate in the Portals Admin Center
Audit web role assignments quarterly	Prevents privilege accumulation over time	Review the Web Roles subgrid on Contact records; use Dataverse Advanced Find
Test with role-specific accounts	Catches permission gaps before real users encounter them	Create test contacts with each web role; test in private browser windows

Deployment Checklist

Going live with a Power Pages site is not simply a matter of clicking Publish. A site that looks complete in a developer environment can harbor hidden issues, misconfigured authentication, unlicensed capacity, missing custom domain settings, or forms that work perfectly in a sandbox but fail under real-world load. Working through a structured checklist before go-live removes the most common causes of a troubled launch.

Go-Live Readiness Checks

Authentication and Security

- All identity providers have been registered and tested with production-level credentials, not development or trial app registrations.

- Redirect URIs in the identity provider app registration match the production site URL exactly, including the correct subdomain and custom domain if applicable.

- Local authentication password policy settings meet your organization's security standards.

- All custom web roles have been reviewed and assigned only the minimum required table permissions.

- Column permissions have been applied to any tables containing sensitive fields.

- The site has been tested in anonymous mode to confirm that no unintended data is exposed.

- DLP policies covering the production environment have been reviewed.

Custom Domain and SSL

- A custom domain has been configured rather than the default *.powerappsportals.com subdomain, if required by your organization.

- A valid SSL certificate has been uploaded or the managed certificate option is in use.

- The DNS CNAME record points correctly to the Power Pages site.

- HTTPS enforcement is enabled; the site should redirect all HTTP traffic to HTTPS automatically.

Licensing

- The site has been assessed against the Power Pages licensing model: authenticated page views and anonymous page views are tracked separately.

- The correct capacity add-ons have been purchased or assigned to the environment.

- If the site will run on a Dynamics 365 license entitlement, the entitlement tier covers the expected number of authenticated users.

- A license review has been scheduled for 90 days after go-live to account for actual usage patterns.

Performance

- The site has been load-tested with a realistic concurrent user count.

- Large Dataverse queries in lists have been filtered and paginated rather than returning all records.

- Static assets such as images, CSS, and JavaScript files are optimized for size.

- The Content Delivery Network (CDN) option is enabled in the Portals Admin Center if your user base is geographically distributed.

Content and UX

- All pages have been reviewed for spelling, broken links, and placeholder text.

- Error pages, 404, 403, and 500, have been customized to show your organization's branding rather than the default system pages.

- The site renders correctly on mobile devices and in the browsers your users are most likely to use.

- The organization's required accessibility standard, such as WCAG 2.1 AA where applicable.

Table 5-5 consolidates the full go-live checklist into a single reference you can work through before publishing your site to production.

Table 5-5. *Power Pages Go-Live Checklist*

Checklist Area	Item	Status
Authentication	Identity providers use production app registrations	Pending/Complete
Authentication	Redirect URIs match production domain	Pending/Complete
Security	Web roles reviewed and scoped correctly	Pending/Complete
Security	Anonymous access tested, no unintended data exposure	Pending/Complete
Domain and SSL	Custom domain configured and DNS verified	Pending/Complete
Domain and SSL	SSL certificate valid and HTTPS enforced	Pending/Complete
Licensing	Page view capacity confirmed for expected volume	Pending/Complete
Performance	Large queries paginated and filtered	Pending/Complete
Performance	CDN enabled for geographically distributed users	Pending/Complete
Content	No placeholder text or broken links remain	Pending/Complete
Content	Custom error pages configured	Pending/Complete

ALM for Power Pages

Application Lifecycle Management (ALM) is the practice of managing the full journey of a solution from development through testing and into production. In the context of Power Pages, ALM means keeping your development work in a separate environment, promoting it through a test environment for validation, and then deploying only approved, tested configurations to production.

Without ALM practices, teams end up making changes directly in production, which carries significant risk. A broken form, a misconfigured permission, or an accidental site settings change can immediately affect real users with no straightforward way to roll back quickly.

Solution-Aware Power Pages

Power Pages is solution-aware, which means site configurations are stored as solution components in Dataverse and can be packaged into a Power Platform solution. The components that travel in a solution include site settings, web templates, page templates, web files, content snippets, entity lists, entity forms, web roles, and table permissions, essentially everything that defines how a site behaves.

What does not travel in a solution are data records themselves. Solutions carry configuration, not data.

Recommended Environment Structure

- **Development:** Where builders create and test new features. This environment has a full copy of the site configuration but typically minimal or anonymized data.

- **Test and UAT:** Where stakeholders and testers validate new features against realistic data before they reach real users. Configuration is promoted here via a managed solution.

- **Production:** The live environment serving real users. Changes should only reach production after passing through test. The site configuration here is installed as a managed solution, meaning it cannot be edited directly.

Moving Solutions Between Environments

Step by Step: Exporting and Importing a Power Pages Solution

1. **Create or Locate the Solution:** In your development environment, navigate to make.powerpages.microsoft.com

and then Solutions. If a solution does not already exist for this
site, create one. Open the solution and verify that your site
components are included.

2. **Add Site Components to the Solution:** From the solution, choose
    Add existing and select the Power Pages site. The wizard will guide
    you in selecting which site subcomponents to include.

3. **Set the Solution Version:** In the solution properties, increment
    the version number, for example, from 1.0.0.0 to 1.1.0.0, to reflect
    the changes being deployed. Good version control habits make it
    much easier to track what changed and when.

4. **Export the Solution as Managed:** In the Solutions list, select your
    solution, click Export, choose Managed, and download the .zip
    file. Managed solutions prevent accidental direct editing in target
    environments.

5. **Import into the Target Environment:** In the test or production
    environment, navigate to Solutions then Import. Upload the
    .zip file, review the import summary, and click Import. Power
    Pages will apply the configuration changes without affecting data
    records.

6. **Verify the Deployment:** After import, open the site and test key
    user journeys, sign-in, form submission, list rendering, to confirm
    the deployment has not introduced any regressions.

7. **Use the Power Platform CLI for Automation:** For teams
    operating a CI/CD pipeline, the pac solution export and pac
    solution import commands automate these steps. Integrate
    them into a GitHub Actions or Azure DevOps pipeline for fully
    automated promotion between environments.

Table 5-6 summarizes the key ALM activities for Power Pages, the recommended tool
or method for each, and important notes to guide your approach.

Table 5-6. *ALM Activities and Tools for Power Pages*

ALM Activity	Tool or Method	Notes
Export site configuration	Power Pages Studio, Solutions or Power Platform CLI (pac solution export)	Always export as Managed for target environments
Import configuration	Power Platform Admin Center, Solutions, Import, or pac solution import	Review the import log for warnings before verifying site behavior
Version control of solution files	GitHub or Azure DevOps repository	Commit unpacked solution files to source control after each export
Automated CI/CD pipeline	GitHub Actions or Azure DevOps with the pac CLI	Reduces human error and enables rollback via source control
Environment variable management	Environment Variables in the solution	Store endpoint URLs and configuration values as variables to avoid hardcoding per-environment values

Monitoring and Maintenance

A live Power Pages site needs regular attention. Even a site that launched without problems can develop performance issues as data volumes grow, configuration can drift if multiple people have access to the Portal Management app, and errors can accumulate silently unless you are actively monitoring for them.

Using the Power Pages Admin Center

The Power Pages admin center, accessible from admin.powerplatform.microsoft.com or directly from the Power Pages site list by selecting Manage, is the primary tool for monitoring and administering a live site. It consolidates diagnostics, capacity information, custom domain management, and site-level settings in one place.

Key Areas of the Admin Center

- **Site Actions:** Restart the site, enable or disable it, place it in maintenance mode, and manage the site state. Restarting the site clears the server-side cache, useful if configuration changes are not being reflected.

- **Portal Details:** Shows the current site URL, the Dataverse environment it is linked to, and the current site version.

- **Site Health:** Provides a diagnostic view highlighting configuration issues, such as missing web roles on forms, site settings that are incorrectly set, or authentication providers with expired credentials.

- **Performance:** Shows page view counts and can surface pages with unusually high load times. Use this to identify queries that need optimization.

- **Content Delivery Network (CDN):** Toggle the CDN on or off, view CDN status, and purge cached content when you need static changes to be visible immediately.

- **Custom Domains:** Manage SSL certificates, configure custom hostnames, and verify DNS records.

- **IP Address Restrictions:** Restrict access to the site to specific IP ranges, useful for internal-only sites or during a testing phase before public launch.

Monitoring Site Health and Errors

Power Pages logs diagnostic events that can help you identify and resolve problems before users report them.

Portal Trace Logs

Liquid template errors, plugin execution failures, and authentication issues are captured in Portal Trace Logs, which are stored in Dataverse under the Portal Trace Log table. You can view these records in the Portal Management app or query them directly with

Dataverse Advanced Find. Enable verbose logging through the site setting Diagnostics/ TraceLevel, set this to Verbose in development and Error in production to reduce storage consumption.

Power Platform Activity Logging

For organizations subject to audit or compliance requirements, the Microsoft 365 Compliance Center captures Power Platform activity events including Power Pages sign-in activity, data access events, and administrative changes. These logs are retained for 90 days by default. Integrate these with your organization's SIEM tool, such as Microsoft Sentinel, for long-term retention and alerting.

Application Insights Integration

Power Pages sites can be connected to Azure Application Insights for richer telemetry. Once configured through the site setting Diagnostics/ ApplicationInsightsInstrumentationKey, Application Insights will receive page view events, custom events, exceptions, and dependency calls. This enables you to build dashboards showing real-time error rates, user flow analysis, and geographic usage patterns, all in a familiar Azure monitoring experience.

Routine Maintenance Tasks

- **Clear the server-side cache** after significant configuration changes, using Site Actions then Restart in the admin center.

- **Review capacity consumption monthly.** Check authenticated and anonymous page view consumption against your license entitlements to avoid overages.

- **Rotate client secrets and certificates** before they expire. Identity provider app registrations and SSL certificates both have expiry dates. An expired certificate takes the site offline; an expired client secret breaks authentication.

- **Archive or delete stale Contact records** that have web role assignments but no longer need portal access, to keep role assignment data clean.

- **Review and update web templates and content snippets** when your organization's branding, legal notices, or terms of use change.

Troubleshooting and Support

Even well-configured Power Pages sites encounter problems. Authentication failures, permission errors, form submission issues, and page rendering problems are among the most frequently reported issues on live sites. Knowing how to diagnose these quickly saves hours of frustration and limits the impact on your users.

Common Deployment Issues and Resolutions

Table 5-7 covers the most common issues encountered on live Power Pages sites, the likely cause behind each one, and the recommended resolution steps.

Table 5-7. *Common Power Pages Issues and Resolutions*

Issue	Likely Cause	Resolution
Users cannot sign in, authentication error after redirect	Redirect URI in the identity provider app registration does not match the site URL exactly	Verify the redirect URI in the Azure, Google, or OAuth console. Ensure protocol, subdomain, and path all match precisely. Check for trailing slashes.
Users are redirected to sign-in even after authenticating	Contact record not being matched, identity provider email does not match a Contact email in Dataverse	Check whether a Contact exists with the user's email. Review the site setting Authentication/Registration/Enabled.
Form submissions result in a 403 Forbidden error	The web role for the signed-in user does not have Create permission on the target table	Check Table Permissions for the relevant table. Ensure the web role has Create access and the scope is configured correctly.
A list shows no records even though data exists in Dataverse	Table permission scope does not match the data structure	Open the Table Permission record and verify the relationship name for Contact or Account scope. Test with a Global scope temporarily to confirm the table has data.
Custom domain shows a certificate error	SSL certificate has expired or the DNS CNAME has not propagated	Renew the certificate in the admin center. Use a DNS propagation tool to verify the CNAME record globally.
Site configuration changes are not visible after import	Managed solution import completed but server-side cache still serves the old configuration	In the Power Pages admin center, use Site Actions then Restart to clear the cache.
Portal Trace Log shows Liquid rendering error	A web template or content snippet contains invalid Liquid syntax, often after a manual edit	Open the affected web template in the Portal Management app. Review the Liquid code for syntax errors such as unclosed tags or incorrect object names.
Users report intermittent 500 errors on form submission	A plugin or Power Automate flow triggered by the form submission is failing	Review the Plugin Trace Log table in Dataverse and check Power Automate run history for flows triggered by the relevant table.

Diagnostic Tools and Support Paths

Built-In Diagnostics

- **Site Health in the Admin Center:** Run the built-in health check first. It catches many common configuration issues automatically.

- **Portal Trace Logs:** Review these for Liquid, plugin, and authentication errors. Filter by Timestamp and Trace Type to narrow down to the relevant time window.

- **Browser Developer Tools:** Use the Network tab in your browser's developer tools to inspect failed HTTP requests. A 401 response indicates an authentication problem; a 403 indicates a permissions problem; a 500 indicates a server-side error.

- **Power Automate Run History:** For form submission failures, check whether the flow triggered by the form ran and, if so, what error it returned.

Microsoft Support and Community Resources

- **Microsoft Learn Documentation:** docs.microsoft.com/power-pages is the primary reference. It is updated regularly and covers known issues.

- **Power Pages Community Forum:** The Power Pages community at powerusers.microsoft.com is an active forum where most common issues have already been discussed and solved.

- **Microsoft Support:** For production-impacting issues, raise a support request through the Microsoft 365 Admin Center or the Power Platform Admin Center. Provide the site URL, environment ID, and trace log excerpts to accelerate diagnosis.

- **Power Platform Ideas:** ideas.powerapps.com allows you to submit and vote on product improvement suggestions for Power Pages.

Tip   When raising a support request, always include the environment ID found in the Power Platform Admin Center under Environments, the site's unique ID from the admin center, and a description of the exact steps that reproduce the issue. The more specific your submission, the faster you will receive a useful response.

Practice Exercise

The following exercises help you put into practice the security and deployment concepts covered in this chapter. Work through them in sequence to build confidence in configuring authentication, web roles, table permissions, and monitoring for a Power Pages site.

Exercise 1: Configure Web Roles and Table Permissions

In this exercise, you will create a custom web role and configure table permissions so that authenticated contacts can only read their own records from a custom Dataverse table.

1. Open the **Portal Management app** for your site and navigate to Security then Web Roles.

2. Create a new web role named **Site Member**. Leave Authenticated Users Role and Anonymous Users Role both set to No.

3. Navigate to Security then Table Permissions and create a new record. Name it **Member, Read Own Records**.

4. Set the **Scope to Contact** and the **Access Type to Read only**. Select the lookup column that links your table back to the Contact record.

5. In the Web Roles subgrid on the Table Permission record, add the **Site Member** role you created in step 2.

6. Assign the **Site Member** role to a test Contact record, then sign in to the site as that contact in a private browser window.

7. Verify that the list on your site shows only the records that belong to that contact, and that records belonging to other contacts are not visible.

Goal: Confirm that Contact-scoped table permissions correctly restrict data visibility to the signed-in user's own records.

Exercise 2: Run a Pre-Deployment Security Check

In this exercise, you will use the Power Pages admin center and a private browser window to perform a pre-go-live security validation, confirming that anonymous users cannot access data they should not see and that your authentication provider is working correctly in a non-development context.

1. Open the **Power Pages admin center** for your site and run the **Site Health** diagnostic. Note any warnings or errors reported.

2. Open a **private browser window** and navigate to your site URL without signing in. Attempt to access a page that should be restricted to authenticated users and confirm you are redirected to the sign-in page.

3. Attempt to call a Dataverse table through the Power Pages **Web API** as an anonymous user (e.g., using the browser address bar: yoursite.powerappsportals.com/_api/tablename). Confirm you receive a 403 Forbidden response rather than data.

4. Sign in using your configured **authentication provider** (Azure AD B2C, Google, or local). Confirm the sign-in completes successfully and that you land on the correct post-login page.

5. Check the **Portal Trace Log** table in Dataverse for any errors generated during your test session. Investigate and resolve any entries with a Trace Type of Error.

6. Review your go-live checklist (Table 5-5) and mark off each item that you have verified. Identify any remaining items that need attention before the site is published.

Goal: Complete a structured pre-launch security check that confirms anonymous data access is blocked, authentication is working, and no critical configuration errors remain in the Portal Trace Log.

Chapter Summary

This chapter has taken you through the full security and operational lifecycle of a Power Pages site, from initial security design through to live monitoring and problem resolution.

You began by understanding the layered security model, authentication, web role authorization, and table and column permissions, and how the principle of least privilege should guide every configuration decision. You then walked through the setup of the three most common authentication providers: Azure AD B2C for customer-facing sites, OAuth 2.0 social providers for lower-assurance scenarios, and local authentication for simpler use cases.

With authentication in place, you configured web roles and table permissions at the level of detail that production sites require, including the use of column permissions to restrict sensitive fields and scope settings to ensure contacts can only see data that belongs to them. You also explored a set of data security best practices, enforcing server-side validation, applying DLP policies, and auditing role assignments regularly, that protect your site beyond the minimum configuration.

The second half of the chapter addressed operations. You worked through a structured go-live checklist covering authentication, domain and SSL configuration, licensing, performance, and content readiness. You then examined ALM practices for moving site configurations between development, test, and production environments using Power Platform solutions and the CLI, practices that reduce risk and make deployments repeatable.

The chapter closed with a tour of the Power Pages admin center for monitoring, a look at trace logs and Application Insights integration for error detection, and a practical reference table of the most common deployment problems and how to resolve them.

With the knowledge from this chapter, you are equipped to build Power Pages sites that are not only functional and well-designed, but also secure, maintainable, and ready for the demands of a production environment.

Power Pages Troubleshooting Checklist

This appendix provides a structured diagnostic framework for identifying and resolving common issues in Microsoft Power Pages environments. The checklist is organized by problem category and aligned with real-world deployment and production scenarios.

Site Provisioning and Environment Issues

Site Not Provisioned

Symptoms:

- Power Pages site does not appear in the environment.
- Provisioning status remains "In Progress" for extended time.
- Error displayed during site creation.

Checklist:

- ☐ Confirm correct Power Platform environment is selected
- ☐ Verify environment type (Sandbox/Production) supports Power Pages
- ☐ Ensure Dataverse is enabled for the environment
- ☐ Validate sufficient capacity (Database and File capacity)
- ☐ Check user has System Administrator or appropriate environment role

© Dr. Gomathi S, Jerald Felix 2026
Dr. Gomathi S and J. Felix, *Getting Started with Microsoft Power Pages*,
https://doi.org/10.1007/979-8-8688-2667-2

☐ Review Power Platform Admin Center → Environments →
Resources

☐ Retry provisioning from Power Pages home

Escalation:

If provisioning fails repeatedly, raise a Microsoft support ticket with environment ID and
correlation ID.

Incorrect Environment Configuration

Checklist:

☐ Confirm region alignment (Environment region vs. Microsoft
Entra ID tenant region)

☐ Verify environment is not expired (Trial environments)

☐ Ensure correct licensing is assigned to the user

☐ Confirm Dataverse language settings are correct

Authentication and Identity Issues

Authentication is one of the most common failure points in Power Pages
implementations.

Users Unable to Sign In

Symptoms:

- Login page loads but authentication fails.

- Redirect loop after login.

- "Access Denied" error after successful authentication.

Checklist:

☐ Verify identity provider configuration in Set Up → Identity
Providers

- ☐ Confirm correct Client ID and Client Secret
- ☐ Validate Redirect URI matches Microsoft Entra ID/external provider configuration
- ☐ Check token issuer URL
- ☐ Ensure authentication is enabled in Site Settings
- ☐ Verify cookies are not blocked in browser
- ☐ Confirm portal URL matches configured reply URL

Microsoft Entra ID Configuration Issues

Checklist:

- ☐ Microsoft Entra ID app registration exists
- ☐ Redirect URI matches exact portal URL
- ☐ API permissions granted and admin consent provided
- ☐ Client secret not expired
- ☐ Correct tenant ID configured

Web Role Assignment Issues

If login succeeds but data is inaccessible:

- ☐ Confirm contact record exists in Dataverse
- ☐ Ensure contact is linked to Microsoft Entra ID identity
- ☐ Assign appropriate Web Role
- ☐ Verify Web Role has corresponding Table Permissions
- ☐ Confirm Web Role is associated with the correct website

Data Visibility and Security Issues
Records Not Displaying in Lists or Forms

Checklist:

- ☐ Confirm table permission exists
- ☐ Verify table permission scope (Global, Contact, Account, Self)
- ☐ Validate relationship configuration for Contact-scoped permissions
- ☐ Ensure Web Role is assigned to the user
- ☐ Confirm correct table is referenced in List configuration
- ☐ Check FetchXML query syntax
- ☐ Verify records exist in Dataverse
- ☐ Ensure required columns are included in the form

Form Submission Errors

Symptoms:

- Form does not save.
- "Insufficient Permissions" message.
- Validation error without explanation.

Checklist:

- ☐ Confirm Create/Write permission exists
- ☐ Verify required fields are included
- ☐ Validate business rules in Dataverse
- ☐ Check plugins or Power Automate flows triggered on save
- ☐ Review browser console for JavaScript errors
- ☐ Confirm table permission allows Create operation

Column-Level Security Conflicts

☐ Confirm column security profile settings

☐ Verify user profile assignment

☐ Ensure column is not restricted in Dataverse

Liquid and FetchXML Issues

Liquid Not Rendering

Checklist:

☐ Confirm Liquid syntax is valid

☐ Check for unclosed tags

☐ Ensure correct object reference (user, request, entity)

☐ Validate variable names

☐ Confirm template is linked to page

FetchXML Returning No Results

☐ Validate entity logical name

☐ Confirm correct attribute names

☐ Check filter conditions

☐ Ensure user has read permission

☐ Test query directly in Dataverse Advanced Find

Performance and Optimization Issues

Slow Page Load

Checklist:

☐ Optimize image sizes

☐ Minimize large JavaScript libraries

☐ Reduce FetchXML complexity

☐ Enable caching where applicable

☐ Remove unused Web Files

☐ Avoid excessive synchronous API calls

☐ Monitor network requests in browser DevTools

Portal Rendering Delays

☐ Check Dataverse performance

☐ Review Power Automate flows triggered on load

☐ Validate custom plugins execution time

☐ Confirm no blocking JavaScript

Deployment and ALM Issues

Solution Import Errors

Checklist:

☐ Validate dependency components

☐ Confirm environment variables configured

☐ Ensure required tables exist

☐ Check version compatibility

☐ Resolve missing web templates

PAC CLI Upload/Download Errors

☐ Confirm authentication using pac auth list

☐ Verify correct environment selected

☐ Ensure CLI version is latest

☐ Validate folder structure

☐ Confirm network connectivity

Portal Metadata Sync Issues

☐ Confirm portal components included in solution

☐ Verify website binding

☐ Check publishing status

☐ Restart portal from Admin Center if required

Custom Domain and DNS Issues

Custom Domain Not Working

Checklist:

☐ DNS CNAME correctly mapped

☐ SSL certificate provisioned

☐ Domain ownership validated

☐ DNS propagation completed

☐ Check Azure Front Door configuration (if applicable)

Browser and Client-Side Issues
JavaScript Errors

- ☐ Inspect browser console
- ☐ Confirm Web File path correct
- ☐ Check script loading order
- ☐ Validate jQuery dependency (if used)

Cache Issues

- ☐ Clear browser cache
- ☐ Use incognito mode
- ☐ Force refresh (Ctrl + F5)
- ☐ Invalidate CDN cache if enabled

Governance and Licensing Issues
Licensing Errors

- ☐ Confirm user license assignment
- ☐ Verify capacity-based licensing
- ☐ Check environment capacity consumption
- ☐ Review billing status

Escalation Readiness Checklist

Before raising a Microsoft support ticket:

- ☐ Environment ID documented
- ☐ Website ID documented

☐ Correlation ID captured

☐ Exact error message recorded

☐ Screenshots collected

☐ Steps to reproduce documented

☐ Browser console logs exported

Structured Diagnostic Approach

When troubleshooting Power Pages issues, follow this order:

1. Environment validation

2. Authentication validation

3. Web role verification

4. Table permission validation

5. FetchXML testing

6. Browser console inspection

7. Solution and ALM review

This structured order reduces time to resolution and prevents unnecessary configuration changes.

Glossary of Terms

This glossary defines key technical and functional terms used throughout this book. Definitions are aligned with Microsoft Power Pages, Dataverse, and broader Power Platform terminology to support both practitioners and certification candidates.

A

Access Control

Mechanism used to restrict or grant user permissions to portal content, data, and features through Web Roles and Table Permissions.

ALM (Application Lifecycle Management)

A structured approach for managing development, testing, deployment, and maintenance of Power Pages solutions across environments.

Authentication

The process of verifying the identity of a user attempting to access a Power Pages site.

Authorization

The process of determining what an authenticated user is allowed to access or perform.

Microsoft Entra ID (Microsoft Entra ID)

Microsoft's cloud-based identity and access management service used for authentication and user management.

© Dr. Gomathi S, Jerald Felix 2026
Dr. Gomathi S and J. Felix, *Getting Started with Microsoft Power Pages*,
https://doi.org/10.1007/979-8-8688-2667-2

B

Basic Form (Entity Form)

A Power Pages component that allows users to create, view, or edit Dataverse records through a portal interface.

Business Rule

A Dataverse configuration tool that enforces logic at the table level without requiring code.

C

Caching

A performance optimization mechanism that stores frequently accessed data temporarily to reduce load times.

Canvas App

A Power Apps application where the UI is designed manually with drag-and-drop components.

Client ID

A unique identifier assigned to an application registered in Microsoft Entra ID for authentication purposes.

Column-Level Security

A Dataverse security feature that restricts access to specific columns within a table.

Connection Reference

A solution component that stores references to external connections used by flows or apps.

Custom Domain

A personalized domain name mapped to a Power Pages site instead of the default *.powerappsportals.com URL.

D

Dataverse

Microsoft's secure, scalable data platform that stores structured business data for Power Platform applications.

Deployment Pipeline

A structured environment promotion process (Dev → Test → Production) using solutions.

Design Studio

The visual development interface used to build and customize Power Pages sites.

DNS (Domain Name System)

System that translates domain names into IP addresses for internet routing.

E

Environment

A logical container within Power Platform used to store apps, data, flows, and portals.

Environment Variables

Reusable configuration values stored within solutions to support multi-environment deployments.

Entity

Legacy term for a Dataverse Table.

F

FetchXML

An XML-based query language used to retrieve data from Dataverse.

Flow (Power Automate)

An automation process that triggers actions based on defined events.

G

Global Table Permission

A permission type that allows access to all records within a Dataverse table.

H

HTML Web Template

A reusable layout file combining HTML and Liquid used to structure portal pages.

I

Identity Provider

An authentication service (such as Microsoft Entra ID or Google) used to validate user credentials.

Import Solution

Process of deploying packaged solution components into a target environment.

J

JavaScript Web File

A static file uploaded to Power Pages to extend client-side functionality.

L

Liquid

A server-side templating language used in Power Pages to dynamically render data.

List (Entity List)

A component used to display Dataverse records in a tabular format.

M

Managed Solution

A packaged solution used for deployment to test or production environments where editing is restricted.

Model-Driven App

A Power Apps application built primarily on Dataverse data models and business logic.

P

PAC CLI (Power Platform Command Line Interface)

A command-line tool used to manage Power Platform resources, including Power Pages.

Portal Management App

The administrative interface used to configure advanced Power Pages components.

Power Pages

A low-code platform within Power Platform used to build secure external-facing business websites.

Power Platform

Microsoft's suite of low-code tools including Power Apps, Power Automate, Power BI, Dataverse, and Power Pages.

Provisioning

The process of creating and configuring a Power Pages site within an environment.

R

Record-Level Security

Security mechanism that controls access to individual Dataverse records.

Relationship (Dataverse)

A defined connection between two Dataverse tables (1:N, N:1, N:N).

Responsive Design

A design approach ensuring websites adapt to different screen sizes and devices.

S

Security Role

A Dataverse role that controls user permissions within the environment.

Site Setting

A configuration record in Power Pages that controls system-level behavior.

Solution

A container used to package Power Platform components for deployment.

SSL Certificate

A digital certificate used to secure data transmission over HTTPS.

T

Table

A structured data object in Dataverse containing rows (records) and columns.

Table Permission

A security rule in Power Pages that defines access to Dataverse tables for portal users.

Trial Environment

A temporary environment created for evaluation or testing purposes.

U

Unmanaged Solution

A solution used in development environments that allows editing and customization.

User (Contact Record)

A portal user represented by a Contact record in Dataverse.

W

Web File

A static resource such as JavaScript, CSS, or images uploaded to Power Pages.

Web Role

A security role assigned to portal users to control access to pages and data.

Website Record

A Dataverse record representing a Power Pages site configuration.

Learning Path to Certifications Relevant to Power Pages

This appendix outlines the Microsoft certifications that directly support a career in Power Pages development, configuration, architecture, and governance.

Power Pages is part of the **Power Platform ecosystem**, and therefore the most relevant certifications fall under the **AI Business Solutions → Power Platform track**.

Foundation Level

PL-900

Microsoft Power Platform Fundamentals

Level: Fundamentals

Why It Matters for Power Pages:

- Introduces Dataverse concepts

- Covers security basics

- Explains Power Pages capabilities

- Provides overview of authentication and environments

Who Should Take It:

- Beginners

- Functional consultants

Dr. Gomathi S and J. Felix, *Getting Started with Microsoft Power Pages*,
https://doi.org/10.1007/979-8-8688-2667-2

- Students

- Career transition professionals

PL-900 is the recommended starting point before moving into specialization.

Core Functional Certification

PL-200

Power Platform Functional Consultant Associate

Level: Associate

This is the most important certification for Power Pages professionals.

Skills Covered:

- Dataverse table design

- Relationships and data modeling

- Security roles and permissions

- Table permissions

- Authentication configuration

- Requirements gathering

- Solution configuration

Power Pages Relevance:

- Web roles

- Table permissions

- Portal configuration

- Identity providers

- Environment planning

Recommended For:

- Functional consultants

- Power Pages implementers

- Business solution designers

Developer-Level Certification

PL-400

Power Platform Developer Associate

Level: Associate

Essential for technical Power Pages developers.

Skills Covered:

- JavaScript customization

- Web API integration

- Custom connectors

- Plugins

- Azure integration

- Application Lifecycle Management (ALM)

- CLI usage

Power Pages Relevance:

- Liquid templates

- FetchXML

- JavaScript web files

- Advanced portal customization

- DevOps deployment

- PAC CLI usage

Recommended For:

- Developers

- Technical consultants

- Integration specialists

Expert-Level Certification

PL-600

Power Platform Solution Architect Expert

Level: Expert

This certification validates enterprise-level architecture skills.

Skills Covered:

- Solution design

- Governance strategy

- Security architecture

- Environment strategy

- Scalability planning

- Integration architecture

Power Pages Relevance:

- Multi-environment portal deployment

- Enterprise authentication strategy

- Security design blueprint

- Performance and scalability

- Governance and compliance

Recommended For:

- Senior consultants

Architects

- Enterprise solution designers

Recommended Certification Sequence for Power Pages

Functional Track:

PL-900 → PL-200 → PL-600

Developer Track:

PL-900 → PL-200 → PL-400 → PL-600

Beginner Track:

PL-900 → PL-200

Certification-to-Role Mapping

Certification	Role Alignment
PL-900	Power Platform Beginner
PL-200	Power Pages Functional Consultant
PL-400	Power Pages Developer
PL-600	Power Platform Solution Architect

Common Power Pages Interview Questions

This appendix provides commonly asked interview questions for Power Pages professionals across functional, technical, and architectural roles. Questions are grouped by experience level and role focus.

Fundamental-Level Questions (0–2 Years)

1. **What is Microsoft Power Pages?**

   Power Pages is a low-code platform within Microsoft Power Platform used to build secure, external-facing business websites integrated with Dataverse.

2. **What is Dataverse and how does it relate to Power Pages?**

   Dataverse is the data platform used to store structured business data. Power Pages uses Dataverse tables to display, create, and manage data through portal interfaces.

3. **What is a Web Role?**

   A Web Role is a security role assigned to portal users (Contacts) that controls access to pages and data within Power Pages.

4. **What is a Table Permission?**

   A Table Permission defines access (Create, Read, Update, Delete) to Dataverse tables for portal users based on scope.

© Dr. Gomathi S, Jerald Felix 2026
Dr. Gomathi S and J. Felix, *Getting Started with Microsoft Power Pages,*
https://doi.org/10.1007/979-8-8688-2667-2

5. **What are the different Table Permission scopes?**

   - Global

   - Contact

   - Account

   - Self

6. **What is the difference between a Security Role and a Web Role?**

   Security Roles apply to internal users in Dataverse.

   Web Roles apply to external users accessing Power Pages.

7. **What is a Basic Form?**

   A Basic Form allows portal users to create, edit, or view a single Dataverse record.

8. **What is a List in Power Pages?**

   A List displays multiple Dataverse records in a tabular format on the portal.

Functional Consultant-Level Questions (2–5 Years)

1. **How do you configure authentication in Power Pages?**

   Authentication is configured using Identity Providers such as Microsoft Entra ID. The process includes

   - App registration in Microsoft Entra ID

   - Configuring Client ID and secret

   - Setting redirect URI

   - Enabling authentication in portal settings

2. **How do you restrict data so users see only their own records?**

   Use Table Permissions with Contact scope and ensure proper relationship between Contact and the table.

3. **What is the relationship between Contact records and portal users?**

   Each portal user is represented by a Contact record in Dataverse. Web Roles are assigned to the Contact.

4. **How would you design security for a vendor portal?**

- Create Web Roles per vendor type

- Configure Table Permissions with Account scope

- Restrict data visibility using relationships

- Implement authentication via Microsoft Entra ID or B2C

5. **What are Site Settings?**

Site Settings are configuration records that control system-level behavior in Power Pages.

6. **How do you migrate a Power Pages solution to production?**

- Use managed solutions

- Include portal components in the solution

- Configure environment variables

- Deploy using solution import or PAC CLI

Developer-Level Questions (3–7 Years)

1. **What is Liquid in Power Pages?**

Liquid is a server-side templating language used to dynamically render Dataverse data within portal pages.

2. **What is FetchXML?**

FetchXML is an XML-based query language used to retrieve data from Dataverse.

3. **How is JavaScript used in Power Pages?**

JavaScript enhances client-side functionality such as form validation, UI interactions, and dynamic behaviors.

4. **What is PAC CLI and why is it important?**

PAC CLI (Power Platform Command Line Interface) is used for managing solutions and portal metadata, enabling DevOps and automated deployments.

5. **How do you optimize performance in Power Pages?**

- Reduce complex FetchXML queries

- Enable caching

- Minimize JavaScript libraries

- Optimize images

- Reduce API calls

6. **What are common causes of "Access Denied" errors?**

- Missing Web Role

- Incorrect Table Permission

- Incorrect scope configuration

- Page permissions

- Relationship misconfiguration

Architect-Level Questions (5+ Years)

1. **How would you design a multi-environment deployment strategy?**

- Separate Dev, Test, and Production environments

- Use unmanaged solutions in Dev

- Use managed solutions in Test/Prod

- Maintain environment variables

- Use PAC CLI or pipelines

2. **How would you design secure external authentication?**

- Use Microsoft Entra ID or Microsoft Entra ID B2C

- Configure redirect URIs correctly

- Enforce HTTPS

- Implement role-based access

- Enable least privilege model

3. **How do you ensure governance in Power Pages implementations?**

- Establish naming conventions
- Define Web Role standards
- Implement environment strategy
- Use solution-based deployments
- Document security model

4. **How would you scale a high-traffic portal?**

- Optimize queries
- Use caching
- Reduce heavy client scripts
- Monitor performance
- Consider CDN for static assets

5. **What are key risks in Power Pages projects?**

- Poor security modeling
- Incorrect Table Permission scope
- Hard-coded environment values
- Lack of ALM strategy
- Improper authentication setup

Scenario-Based Interview Questions

1. **A user can log in but cannot see any records. What would you check?**

- Web Role assignment
- Table Permission existence
- Scope configuration
- Relationship mapping
- Record ownership

2. **How would you design a customer self-service portal?**

- Authentication via Microsoft Entra ID B2C

- Contact-based access

- Case table permissions

- Basic Forms for case creation

- Lists for case tracking

3. **How would you handle integration with external systems?**

- Use Power Automate

- Custom connectors

- Web API

- Azure Functions

Behavioral and Design Questions

1. **How do you handle conflicting security requirements?**

- Conduct requirement analysis

- Design least-privilege model

- Use scope-based permissions

- Validate with testing scenarios

2. **How do you ensure solution maintainability?**

- Follow naming conventions

- Avoid hard-coded values

- Use environment variables

- Maintain documentation

- Use managed deployments

Quick Revision Section

Candidates should be comfortable explaining

- Web Role vs. Security Role

- Table Permission scope types

- Authentication flow

- Contact record mapping

- Managed vs. Unmanaged solutions

- Liquid vs. JavaScript

- ALM lifecycle

Power Pages Production Readiness Checklist

This appendix provides a structured framework to evaluate whether a Power Pages solution is ready for production deployment. It is designed for functional consultants, developers, architects, and DevOps teams responsible for secure and scalable go-live implementations.

This checklist should be completed before moving from Test/UAT to Production.

Environment Readiness

Environment Strategy

- ☐ Development, Test, and Production environments are clearly separated
- ☐ Production environment is not a trial environment
- ☐ Environment region aligns with organizational compliance requirements
- ☐ Proper naming conventions are followed

Capacity Validation

- ☐ Dataverse database capacity reviewed
- ☐ File storage capacity verified
- ☐ Log storage monitored
- ☐ Expected production traffic volume estimated

© Dr. Gomathi S, Jerald Felix 2026
Dr. Gomathi S and J. Felix, *Getting Started with Microsoft Power Pages*,
https://doi.org/10.1007/979-8-8688-2667-2

Solution Packaging

☐ All customizations included in a solution

☐ No unmanaged customizations in production

☐ Managed solution prepared for deployment

☐ Version number incremented properly

Security Readiness

Authentication Configuration

☐ Identity provider configured correctly (Microsoft Entra ID/ Microsoft Entra ID B2C/other)

☐ Client ID and Client Secret validated

☐ Redirect URI matches production domain

☐ HTTPS enforced

☐ Token expiration settings reviewed

Web Role Validation

☐ All required Web Roles created

☐ Web Roles mapped to appropriate Contact records

☐ Anonymous role permissions reviewed

☐ Excess roles removed

Table Permission Validation

☐ Table Permissions created for all exposed tables

☐ Scope (Global/Contact/Account/Self) verified

☐ Relationships validated for scoped access

☐ CRUD permissions reviewed

☐ No unintended global access

Least Privilege Enforcement

☐ Users cannot access unrelated records

☐ Sensitive tables not exposed

☐ Column-level security reviewed

☐ Admin privileges restricted

Data Integrity and Configuration

Data Validation

☐ Required fields enforced

☐ Business rules validated

☐ Lookup relationships tested

☐ Duplicate detection rules reviewed

Contact and Account Model

☐ Portal users mapped correctly to Contact records

☐ Account relationships validated

☐ Ownership model reviewed

Performance Readiness

FetchXML Optimization

☐ Queries tested for performance

☐ Avoided unnecessary joins

☐ Limited returned attributes

☐ Pagination implemented where required

Page Performance

☐ Large images optimized

☐ Unused JavaScript removed

☐ CSS minified

☐ Lazy loading implemented where applicable

Caching Strategy

☐ Portal caching enabled

☐ Cache invalidation tested

☐ No dynamic data unintentionally cached

Application Lifecycle Management (ALM)

Solution Governance

☐ Environment variables configured

☐ Connection references updated

☐ All dependencies resolved

☐ No hard-coded URLs

Deployment Validation

☐ Managed solution imported successfully

☐ Portal metadata synchronized

☐ Web templates validated

☐ Web files uploaded and tested

Rollback Plan

☐ Backup of previous version taken

☐ Clear rollback procedure documented

☐ Data backup verified

☐ Incident escalation plan defined

Domain and SSL Configuration

Custom Domain Setup

☐ DNS CNAME configured

☐ Domain ownership validated

☐ DNS propagation verified

☐ SSL certificate provisioned

HTTPS Enforcement

☐ HTTP redirected to HTTPS

☐ No mixed content warnings

☐ All resources loaded securely

Compliance and Governance

Regulatory Compliance

☐ Data residency requirements verified

☐ Privacy policy updated

☐ Cookie consent configured (if applicable)

☐ Data retention policy documented

Audit and Monitoring

☐ Audit logging enabled

☐ Security monitoring configured

☐ Admin access monitored

☐ Error logging reviewed

Functional Testing Validation

Role-Based Testing

☐ Each Web Role tested independently

☐ Anonymous access tested

☐ Restricted access validated

Form and List Testing

☐ Create functionality tested

☐ Edit functionality tested

☐ Delete functionality tested

☐ Validation messages confirmed

☐ Error handling verified

Edge Case Testing

☐ Expired sessions tested

☐ Invalid login attempts tested

☐ Network interruption scenarios tested

Integration Readiness

☐ Power Automate flows tested

☐ API integrations validated

☐ External services reachable

☐ Timeout handling implemented

Documentation Readiness

☐ Architecture diagram updated

☐ Security model documented

☐ Web Role matrix documented

☐ Deployment steps documented

☐ Admin guide prepared

Go-Live Approval Checklist

Before final production release:

☐ UAT sign-off obtained

☐ Security review approved

☐ Performance testing completed

☐ Stakeholder approval received

☐ Final deployment scheduled

Post-Go-Live Monitoring Plan

☐ Monitor login success rates

☐ Monitor performance metrics

☐ Review error logs daily for first week

☐ Validate data integrity after first batch transactions

☐ Schedule periodic security review

Production Readiness Summary Matrix

Area	Status	Owner	Approved
Environment			
Security			
Performance			
ALM			
Compliance			
Testing			

Recommended Usage

This checklist should be

- Completed during UAT phase
- Reviewed by architect
- Approved by security team
- Signed off before go-live

Index

A

B

C

L

M

S

T

GPSR Compliance
The European Union's (EU) General Product Safety Regulation (GPSR) is a set
of rules that requires consumer products to be safe and our obligations to
ensure this.

If you have any concerns about our products, you can contact us on

ProductSafety@springernature.com

In case Publisher is established outside the EU, the EU authorized
representative is:

Springer Nature Customer Service Center GmbH
Europaplatz 3
69115 Heidelberg, Germany